FULLY
ALIVE

FULLY
ALIVE

Living the Life God Created You to Live

JOHN SHUEY

Published by Webbdezyne.com
Dillsburg, Pennsylvania

Text design and typesetting by Webbdezyne

Cover design by Karen Webb.

ISBN: 978-1500783501

For Worldwide Distribution, Printed in the U.S.A.

1 2 3 4 5 6 / 17 16 15 14

Dedication

There are many people that I would like to dedicate *Fully Alive* to. First, I want to dedicate the book to my daughters, Kristin Bedi and Allison Buzard, their husbands Andrew and Adam and our two precious granddaughters. I love you guys so much.

Secondly, I want to dedicate this book to the many wonderful Christian workers that I have met in various places in the world, who seek to live life for Jesus to its fullest.

The person I want most to dedicate this book to is my wife, Kerry. Kerry, you demonstrate to me day in and day out how to live *Fully Alive*. I have had the opportunity to observe your life for thirty-seven years and you daily exemplify a passion for Jesus, a love for people and dedication to advancing Jesus' Kingdom. Thank you for sharing your life with me and for helping me to be more like Jesus.

Lastly, of course, I want to dedicate *Fully Alive* to the Lord Jesus Christ. Without Him, no one could be *Fully Alive*. Jesus thanks for saving me and being faithful in every circumstance.

Acknowledgments

Fully Alive summarizes over forty years of growth in Jesus. How do you acknowledge everyone who helped you along the way.

I want to thank all of my pastors, seminary professors and those who have helped disciple me since I rededicated my life to Jesus at eighteen years of age. You remain nameless here, but you are each known in heaven for helping me and so many others.

I must also thank my wife, Kerry, who helped forge the material in *Fully Alive* and who helped with the initial editing. Your love and encouragement keep me going.

There have been a number of people who have helped putting the book together. Karen Webb from Webbdezyne has been a great help in encouraging me to go for it, for overseeing the project and for the fun cover design.

I also want to thank my editor, who chose to remain anonymous. I appreciate how you spotted unclear passages, rewrote material to make it more understandable and for the helpful notes that have taught me much about writing.

Each of you has been used by the Lord in bringing this project together.

Thank you!!

Contents

Foreword by David Ravenhill 11

Introduction 13

SECTION I
GOD'S UNRELENTING LOVE

CHAPTER ONE
"Mankind, We Have a Problem!" 21

CHAPTER TWO
God's Plan has Not Changed 35

CHAPTER THREE
Jesus is The One Sent by God 47

CHAPTER FOUR
Fully Alive 63

CHAPTER FIVE
What Makes You Think.... 77

CHAPTER SIX
Law Versus Grace 99

SECTION II
CALLED TO OBEY

CHAPTER SEVEN
Intimacy with God. 117

CHAPTER EIGHT
Commit Your Life Fully to Jesus 131

CHAPTER NINE
Allow God to Remove Hindrances. 149

CHAPTER TEN
Allow the Word to Live in You 171

CHAPTER ELEVEN
Prayer that Changes the World 187

CHAPTER TWELVE
Empowered by the Holy Spirit 203

CHAPTER THIRTEEN
Connect to a Like-Minded, Loving Family 217

CHAPTER FOURTEEN
Discovering Your God-Ordained Destiny. 235
Conclusion 251
Appendix A 253
About the Ministry 257

Foreword

As a grandfather I delight in being with my grandchildren who range from a two-year-old to a twenty-year-old. Naturally the two-year-old does not have the maturity of the twenty-year-old but will, in time, as he develops. I can honestly say I love all of them equally, but I have much more in common with the twenty-year-old due to his age. Sadly, age alone though does not equal maturity. It's possible to be twenty years old and still have the mind of a two-year-old.

In a similar way, there are many believers today who are spiritual babies. This was the apostle Paul's concern for the Corinthian believers. He wrote to them saying, "you have need of milk and not solid food." This was Paul's way of saying that they were undeveloped and had ceased growing spiritually.

As wonderful as children are, they are incapable of functioning in certain areas of responsibility. Most weekends I fly somewhere for a series of speaking engagements. You can imagine my horror if, when boarding the plane, I would glance into the cockpit and see a five-year-old at the controls. No airline in the world would allow a child this degree of authority and responsibility. Given time and training that five-year-old may well take the controls, but only in twenty or thirty years' time.

God as our Father is no respecter of persons and loves the new-born believer as much as any of His other sons and daughters. Like any earthly father, our heavenly Father longs to see His children grow and mature. Only then can He entrust them with the responsibilities of His Kingdom. For this reason we read over and over in the Word of God that we are to press on to maturity, grow in grace, knowledge, love, etc. But how?

Fully Alive answers that question. This book leads you step by step on that journey toward maturity. This is no thriller to be read through and forgotten, but rather a how-to manual to be studied and obeyed. Like any journey there will be times when you feel exhausted or perhaps even discouraged by the lack progress you seem to have made. If that is the case, don't turn back, simply slow down a little. The enemy will always try and drive you while the Lord desires to lead you. The Christian race is not a sprint but a marathon. Remember too that you are not alone, the Holy Spirit is your constant companion, guide and helper.

Just as through eating correctly and proper exercise we develop mentally and physically, the same applies spiritually. *Fully Alive* provides a solid diet for the journey ahead. Obedience to what you read will turn your flab into spiritual muscle and prepare you for your role as a priest and king. With that calling and purpose in mind, keep reading, praying, and obeying, and you will discover what it means to become *fully alive.*

David Ravenhill
Author and Teacher
Siloam Springs, Arkansas

Introduction

When God the Father sent Jesus to earth, He set in motion a movement designed to bring the world under His control. He planned to see an ever-expanding core of disciples who would walk in intimacy with Him, experience the abundant life that He had created humankind to enjoy and tell others how they can experience this life. God longed to bring a sufficient number of people in a locale or nation into this abundant life, that the culture around them would be impacted.

Since the time that Jesus ascended to be with His Father in heaven, hundreds of millions have embraced Him. Currently, 1.3 billion people claim to be Christians. There is a movement of believers in every nation of the world. The world has been touched by His Spirit through His Body. Much of the world's great art, such as the paintings in the Sistine Chapel, and music, such as Handel's Messiah, are a result of the truths of Christianity. The compassion of those who followed Christ opened hospitals to care for the needy, and a hunger for truth by those believing in Christ have resulted in the founding of great educational institutions such as Harvard. There are reports of entire cities being changed for the better because of the impact of Christianity.

A few stories from the Welsh Revival illustrate this fact. For example, a great wave of sobriety swept Scotland. J. Edwin Orr tells how taverns went out of business, and public morals changed. Orr also tells of an interesting phenomenon that happened in the mines—the men were so changed that they stopped using profanity. The pit ponies that carried the coal stood dumbfounded, not knowing what to do because they no longer understood what the men were saying.[1] These are only a few examples of how Scotland and Wales were changed because of Christianity.

Unfortunately, it seems that in the "Christian West," the influence of the Church is waning. To be sure, there are many exceptions to this generalization. Recently my wife and I spoke in a church where a number of people who had been experiencing great difficulty in their lives are now on fire and serving Jesus. The Western Church also continues to send many missionaries, both short-term and long-term, and funds many compassionate relief ministries, such as the Salvation Army, World Vision, and Samaritan's Purse. But sadly, many churches are declining and closing, and many others have little impact.

The good news is, God's plan has never changed. He wants His Church to impact the world. *Fully Alive* outlines how believers in the Lord Jesus Christ can influence those around them, and impact the world. The first six chapters tell us what God desires to accomplish and how He does it. Chapters 7 through 14 tell believers what they can do to be *fully alive,* and have the greatest impact possible.

An Eternal Perspective

Fully Alive examines the life believers can live from the time they ask Christ into their lives until they go to be with Him in eternity.

However, in order to place this in proper perspective, we must address two important biblical issues that place the book in its proper context.

1. We only enter this abundant life by trusting in the blood Jesus shed when He died on the cross to pay the penalty for our sin and rose from the grave victorious over death. Paul told the Romans, *"for all have sinned and fall short of the glory of God"* (Romans 3:23). Later, when Paul described the life of those who had not yet received Jesus Christ to the church in Ephesus, he said, *"...Like the rest, we were by nature deserving of wrath"* (Ephesians 2:3). Our very nature was condemned and we were worthy of judgment. He further told the Romans, *"All have turned away, they have together become worthless; there is no one who does good, not even one"* (Romans 3:12). No one will work their way into a relationship with God or into heaven by their good works. When condemned sinners ask Jesus to forgive their sins and come into their lives, the sin that separated them from God is removed, and the Holy Spirit enters their lives connecting them to God. They come alive spiritually, and for the first time they are *fully alive*— spirit, soul, and body! This new life makes it possible to live life to the fullest.

2. We can experience abundant life on earth, but we will never be more *fully alive* than when we enter into God's eternity:

   He will wipe away every tear from their eyes. There will be no more death or mourning or crying or pain, for the old order of things has passed away (Revelation 21:4).

   So will it be with the resurrection of the dead. The body that is sown is perishable, it is raised imperishable; it is sown in dishonor, it is raised in glory; it is sown in weakness, it is raised in power; it is sown a natural body, it is raised a spiritual body... (1 Corinthians 15:42-44).

...I desire to depart and be with Christ, which is better by far (Philippians 1:23).

We will have an imperishable body with no pain or death, living in the presence of Jesus Himself. It cannot get any better than that! We will be with the angels and the twenty-four elders, gazing at the glorified Jesus and bowing in ecstatic worship to the One who is more amazing than we can currently imagine (Revelation 4 and 5).

Fully Alive focuses on the time between when people receive Jesus Christ into their lives, and when they go to be with Him. It focuses upon the life He has for us during our time on earth. It focuses upon being the kind of person who plays a role in taking the rule of God to the ends of the earth. I want you to see the eternal context in which the principles in this book reside.

You will find that many of the Scripture references come from the Gospel of John. Five years ago, I began a study in First John and quickly realized that I would understand John's thoughts much better if I studied John's Gospel. Consequently, I have studied the Gospel of John for the past five years; it is the inspiration for *Fully Alive*. This is not intended to be a commentary on John's Gospel—there are plenty of good ones out there already. My goal is to capture John's intentions, which are expressed in two key passages:

The thief comes only to steal and kill and destroy; I have come that they may have life, and have it to the full (John 10:10).

Jesus performed many other signs in the presence of his disciples, which are not recorded in this book. But these are written that you may believe that Jesus is the Messiah, the Son of God, and that by believing you may have life in his name (John 20:30-31).

John wanted his readers to experience the life God intended for them. *Fully Alive* has been written to help people discover the abundant life that God intends for them, and how they can live that life by the Holy Spirit's power.

I trust that *Fully Alive* will assist you to live more fully as God intends for you to live. Read it and reread it as God leads you, and may God bless your life and ministry!

ENDNOTE

1. J. Edwin Orr, *The Flaming Tongue* (Chicago: Moody Press, 1973), 17-18.

SECTION I

GOD'S UNRELENTING LOVE

CHAPTER ONE

"Mankind, We Have a Problem!"

Apollo 13 blasted off with the goal of being the third United States manned space mission to the moon. However, the mission did not go as planned. The lunar landing was aborted after an oxygen tank exploded, damaging a crucial part of the mission. After the damage occurred, crewman John L. Swigert Jr. said, "Houston, we've had a problem." These words were later immortalized by Tom Hanks (who played James Lovell in the movie *Apollo 13),* when he said, "Houston, we have a problem."[1] This problem kept the crew from fulfilling the purpose of the mission. The only thing Houston control could do was to try to get the astronauts home safely.

Before NASA made plans to go to the moon, which the Apollo 13 astronauts wanted to explore, God created the heaven and the earth, and He created humanity for an amazing life with the greatest mission ever given.

HE CREATED US IN HIS IMAGE

The earliest record of creation is recorded for us in the biblical Book of Genesis. We are told that after God created much of the universe, including land and sea animals, He said, *"Let us make mankind in our image, in our likeness..."* (Genesis 1:26). John Walton tells us that the ancient people understood the term "image" to mean "to carry the essence of that which it represented."[2] Humankind in the image or essence of God began with great promise. Man became a living being when God breathed His own life into him (Genesis 2:7). This breath of life from God the Father gave man the ability to be like God!

The image of God included three characteristics that gave Adam and Eve, and every human after them, the potential for a fulfilling life. First, God gave humankind intellect. This intellect had a great capacity that enabled Adam to name and know all the animals God had created (Genesis 2:19-20). His created beings' intellect also included the ability to reason. We observe this reasoning in Eve as she interacted with Satan who disguised himself as a snake. She listened to the serpent and weighed what he said, in light of the fact that God had told Adam not to eat the fruit from that tree (Genesis 3:1-6). As she pondered these conflicting statements, she exercised her ability to choose—the second characteristic of the image of God.

Third, God created humans with a capacity to walk intimately with Him. After Adam and Eve ate from the forbidden tree, they heard the sound of God in the garden (Genesis 3:8). They knew this sound because they had heard it before. God had obviously come to the garden to meet them in their past. These encounters with God show us that humankind has the ability to interact with God, and that God desires to have fellowship with humans. The fellowship between God and Adam was clear and specific. For example, God told Adam to name the animals when He brought them to him, and He also told Adam that he could not eat from the tree called, "The tree of good and evil." Even after Adam and Eve ate the forbidden fruit, God communicated directly with them (Genesis 3).

Because God made humankind in His own image, we inherently possessed greatness. There seems to be little limit upon the kind of life we can live as we develop our intellect through experiencing the world God created for us, through hearing God's wisdom and applying our God-given reason and power of choice. From the very beginning of time and conception, God has had a wonderful plan for all humans.

GOD-GIVEN PURPOSE

Not only did God give humankind the potential for full lives, but He also gave us a purpose that gives our lives value and stretches our potential to its limits. After God created man in His image, He told him, *"Be fruitful and increase in number; fill the earth and subdue it. Rule over the fish in the sea and the birds in the sky and over every living creature that moves on the ground."* He later told them, *"I give you every seed-bearing plant on the face of the whole earth and every tree that has fruit with seed in it"* (Genesis 1:28-29).[3] God wanted the entire earth to be under His control. God told Adam to increase in number and bring everything everywhere under His control. Although God could have designed everything so that it was under His control from the moment of creation, He left the work of cultivating plant life, domesticating animal life, and developing a worldwide culture to his vice regents on earth, Adam and Eve and their descendants. God planned a good life for humans, one that would make them *fully alive!*

"MANKIND, WE HAVE A PROBLEM."

However, there was trouble in paradise. God has an enemy, Satan, who did not want to stand by and see God's plan succeed.

The Scriptures tell us that Satan had been a high-ranking, created, heavenly being who wanted to be equal with God, because he was not satisfied to be God's servant. He rebelled against God, so God cast him down to the earth (Isaiah 14:12-14 and Ezekiel 28:11-15). Satan's banishment from heaven did not stop his disdain for God and his desire to spoil His plans. Because of his hatred for God and humankind, Satan showed up at the garden, disguised as a snake, and entered into conversation with Eve. (For me, the conversation would have stopped there. Snakes creep me out, so if one talked to me, I would be out of there!)

As he talked to Eve, he tried to convince her that God had been holding things back from her. He said, "The reason God does not want you to eat from that forbidden fruit is because He knows that if you do eat it, you will be able to determine what is right or wrong on your own." As Eve began to reason, she thought about what it would be like to determine right from wrong using only her reason, which, according to the snake, would be enhanced if she ate from the forbidden tree. As Eve considered her choices, she did not know that the fate of humanity hung in the balance.

Satan knew that if he could deceive Adam and Eve, they would lose their intimacy with God and be cut off from His wisdom. He knew that as humans stumbled through life without God's input in their lives, God's dream for them would be destroyed, His heart would be grieved, and His glory on earth would be reduced. Satan also knew that if Adam and Eve were left to their own reasoning, he would have more opportunities to deceive humankind.

Eve decided that Satan was telling her the truth, ate the forbidden fruit, and persuaded Adam to take a bite. Although they did not die physically, Adam and Eve's life began to change immediately. Prior to eating the forbidden fruit, Adam and Eve walked around naked without shame. Immediately after eating the fruit, Adam and Eve hid from God because they now felt the shame of their disobedience and their inadequacy apart from God. This separation from God proved to be the most devastating blow to humankind because fellowship with God is the greatest privilege known to all humanity. Without this fellowship, humans would be forced to make decisions without God's all-knowing input, which quickly led to some tragic decisions.

In addition to losing their intimacy with God, the Fall[4] also created a schism between Adam and Eve. God told Eve that her desire would be for her husband, and that he would rule over her. The word "desire" in this passage means to possess a desire to dominate. God told Eve that she would no longer be satisfied with her relationship with Adam but that she would desire to control him. God told her, however, that her desire would not be met, but instead she would be ruled by him.[5] There were other changes to Adam and Eve's life: Adam would now cultivate the land with more difficulty, and Eve would experience pain in childbearing (Genesis 3).

As bad as their situation had become, it does not appear that Adam and Eve died. However, Apostle Paul tells us that *"the wages of sin is death"* (Romans 6:23). As we probe deeper, we discover that although Adam and Eve did not die physically (immediately at least), they did die. Isaiah tells us that our sins *"have separated you from your God"* (Isaiah 59:1-2). This separation hindered God from hearing His children's calls for help and keeps Him from using His strength to come to the rescue. Peter tells us that Jesus died *"to bring you to God"* (1 Peter 3:18). As we combine these principles, we discover that the separation from God is death to the spiritual part of a person. After the Fall, the life of God no longer dwelt in the human spirit. Unfortunately, all people live separated from God because of Adam and Eve's sin. The Apostle Paul tells us that death entered the world through one man, Adam. He says, *"in this way death came to all people,"* adding, *"because all sinned"* (Romans 5:12).

There were more changes to Adam and Eve's life because of their decision to seek independence from God. Immediately after the Fall, God whisked Adam and Eve out of the garden, and posted an angel to guard its entrance so they could never enter again. This was not a vindictive act on the part of God. Rather, in love, He did not want them to eat from the other special tree in the garden—the tree of life (Genesis 3:24). God knew that if they ate from the tree of life, in their present state, they would be eternally separated from Him, leading to an eternal spiral into greater and greater depravity.

Recently, we met a couple who decided not to give their young teenage daughter a cell phone. We could look at this as a mean decision that was depriving their daughter. However, being aware of the problems that can happen to teens when they spend a lot time on their phones, like failing to keep up with studies because of social media's addictive power, sexting, and cyber bullying, these parents made their decision because of love. God did the same for Adam and Eve when He removed them from the garden.

The events that followed demonstrated God's wisdom in banishing Adam and Eve from the garden prior to eating fruit from the tree of life. Adam and Eve had two sons. Both sons presented an offering to God. The Lord accepted the sacrifice of Abel, but rejected Cain's sacrifice. Rather than trying to understand and comply with God's standards, Cain killed his brother thinking that he would be acceptable if his brother were not in the picture. In one generation, humans had gone from perfection to murder. They veered far away from God's original intent for them.

A short time later, a man named Lamech killed a young man who sought to harm him. Instead of exhibiting the image of God, humans displayed the character of the destroyer, Satan. Imagine how greatly things would have deteriorated, if humans had been allowed to live eternally in this depraved state. That is why Adam and Eve could not reenter the garden. We must admit that although humankind has made great strides in developing culture through the domestication of animals, the development of manufacturing, composing music, creating art, and other advances, humans cannot change their character. After the Fall, they no longer had the life of God within as in the beginning (Genesis 4). This is true today as well.

I have a friend who works for an engineering company that fulfills contracts for the military. One time he took me along to check on an ongoing project. During our time there, he took me on a tour of one building. The size and capabilities of the machines and weaponry amazed me. Humankind's capacity to invent and our current technological advances are great, yet we have not found a way to curb the violence and immorality that plague our society and world. Humanity, left to our own devices, will continue to fall further down the slippery slope of depravity.

In biblical days, the situation got so bad that *"The Lord saw how great the wickedness of the human race had become on the earth, and that every inclination of the thoughts of the human heart was only evil all the time"* (Genesis 6:5). Men and women had not succeeded in determining right and wrong, but rather had become so depraved that even the inclinations of their hearts had become evil. This evil thinking played right into the hands of Satan. Humans began to respond positively to Satan's evil suggestions because their minds were depraved.

Many years later, Jeremiah tells the Israelites that *"The heart is deceitful above all things and beyond cure. Who can understand it?"* (Jeremiah 17:9). This declaration came at a time when the people of Israel, who had been entrusted with the revealed Scriptures, who had heard the inspired messages of the prophets, and had seen God's miraculous work had abandoned that truth to worship idols instead of serving the Creator. Humans had become so depraved that they could not even trust their own hearts. Tragically, humans can no longer trust that what they perceive to be right or wrong is actually right or wrong. Humans, separated from God, stumble in the darkness.

Paul, the apostle, explains how this happened:

So I tell you this, and insist on it in the Lord, that you must no longer live as the Gentiles do, in the futility of their thinking. They are darkened in their understanding and separated from the life of God because of the ignorance that is in them due to the hardening of their hearts. Having lost all sensitivity, they have given themselves over to sensuality so as to indulge in every kind of impurity, and they are full of greed (Ephesians 4:17-19).

As we look at verse 18, we find Paul making a statement about the condition of the human heart, followed by the reason he found himself in that condition. We must reverse Paul's order to see the proper sequence of events. Let me illustrate. As I write, I am listening to a beautiful piano piece. We may wonder why this pianist plays so well. Someone who knows the artist may tell you that she practices eight hours a day because her teacher told her she had a gift. They continue by telling you that she went to the teacher because she had a great love for music because her mother instilled a love for music in her when she was a very young child. The chronological order of the events that led to the daughter becoming an accomplished pianist is that the mother played beautiful music, which caused the young woman to desire to play. Therefore, she went to the teacher, who told her that she had a gift, motivating her to practice eight hours a day.

We have a similar situation in Paul's words, recorded in Ephesians 4:18. The progression that leads to futile thinking begins with a hardened heart. Say, for example, a man heard God speak and knew what He wanted him do, but the man resisted God's Word causing his heart to be hardened. He did not want to obey God. His desire to disobey God could have been for many reasons. He may have determined that God's request was inconvenient or too hard. He may just have preferred to call the shots in his life. Regardless of the reason, he became hardened. Then he moved to the next step down the spiraling staircase to depravity. He became ignorant. The word "ignorant" actually means to be agnostic. The person reaches the point where he doesn't know if he has heard from God or not. He doesn't know if there is a God.

When people reach this level of depravity, they become darkened in their understanding. In this state they believe what is truly good is bad, and bad is good. For instance, they come to the point of believing that it is good to terminate a pregnancy, thus killing a baby. When people reach this state they find themselves cut off from the life of God. When they are cut off from the life of God, their thinking is useless—the reasoning God gave them is so distorted that they reach the wrong conclusions about life. Their thinking makes the situation worse. No wonder—every inclination of our thoughts is evil continually. We see the result of that type of thinking revealed in Ephesians 4 verse 19.

Those who have gone down this path give themselves over to sensuality in ever-increasing ways. The Old Testament of the Bible is filled with examples of how people's depraved thinking led to sin. The cities of Sodom and Gomorrah were so filled with sexual lust that Lot could not allow visitors to the city to spend the night in the public square. Even in the safety of Lot's home, the men of the city came to engage in sexual relations with the men. Lot offered his daughters to them. Later, after Lot's wife died, his daughters got him drunk two nights in a row so that they might become pregnant by having relations with him (Genesis 19). We find other places where the immorality of the "people of God" reached incredible lows. For instance, we are told of times when the Israelites were defeated militarily, as judgment, because they engaged in immorality with Moabite women (Numbers 25) and we see how immorality spread through the family line of King David because of David's indiscretions (2 Samuel and 1 Kings).

We see this also as we scan the world's religious landscape. We find millions seeking after the nearly 330 million gods in Hinduism, or the more pantheistic approach of Buddhism. In addition, there are more than 1.5 billion people following the god of Islam, Allah. In some of the more tribal areas of the world, the people worship inanimate objects. These religions give many choices to the people of the world that distract them from the God of the Bible. These false religions provide a sense of spirituality that temporarily and ineffectively fill humanity's spiritual void, while keeping people from worshiping the Living God. These religious beliefs have led to a steady stream of people entering eternity without God, while they assumed that they were right with God. Those espousing these philosophies believe that they are solving the world's problems, but they have not done so and their philosophies have not brought them into an intimate relationship with God.

For those who do not believe in God, Satan has blinded their eyes with other types of philosophies. On the political and financial fronts, we have seen radical forms of communism and socialism. Radical socialism, fascism, led to millions being killed in World War II. The early leaders of the communist revolution killed millions and imprisoned others who would not comply with their dictates. Others have sought after the philosophies of materialism and hedonism, which say that the goal of humankind is to increase material possessions and live for pleasure.

Immorality is increasing in our day through human trafficking, often exploiting young boys and girls. There is an increase in pornography, especially on the Internet, where men look at lewd images and women enter into inappropriate relationships through chat rooms in the obscurity of their own homes. Many practices, which were culturally unacceptable just a few decades ago, such as couples living together prior to marriage, same-sex marriages and recreational sex, have become the norm in our society. Some, seeking to go even further, are already setting the table to legitimize polygamy and consensual sexual relations with minors. These philosophies do not produce the freedom people are seeking, but rather take people into greater bondage. Humans separated from God do not live life to its' fullest, but move into greater depravity.

Unfortunately, even those entrusted with the Word of God have missed the truth. As we will discuss in greater detail in later chapters, God the Father sent His Son, the Lord Jesus Christ, to the earth to communicate truth and make it possible for humankind to once again enter into a relationship with God. However, the apostle John tells us, *"He came to that which was his own, but his own did not receive him"* (John 1:11). Jesus Christ created all that is and yet His creation did not recognize Him. The Jewish people had been entrusted with the very words of God spoken through Old Testament prophets. This word was filled with glimpses of the One whom God would send into the world, yet even the majority of Jewish people failed to recognize Him. In fact, as we read the Gospels, we find that the religious leaders who should have known the most about God and His coming One, rejected Him and eventually called for His execution.

As easy as it is for twenty-first century Christians to throw stones at these first century Jewish people, many in the Christian Church have also lost their moral bearings. Recent national surveys related to the cultural and moral issues of our day find no difference between the general population and those who say they believe in the Bible as the Word of God. Unfortunately, there is much immorality, even among "born again" members of Christianity. In addition, marriages break up at nearly the same rate in the Church as the general population. When asked questions that relate to life priorities, we also find that "Christians" in the United States do not differ greatly from those who do not believe the Bible.

Our world is in trouble. Immorality and the threat of nuclear war fill the pages of our newspapers and our Internet news sites. Left to our own devises, our futile, worthless thinking will take us deeper and deeper into depravity, and further from a world ruled by God and the incredible life He has envisioned for us. Instead of a world where humans make wise choices stemming from their intimate fellowship with God, they have depended upon their depraved thinking. The result is the world in which we live—filled with hatred and depression, abuse and rejection, and on the verge of military chaos. We seem to have lost our chance at paradise on earth.

In *Apollo 13,* after the oxygen tank exploded, NASA's Mission Control gladly aborted the mission in order to accomplish the only thing that mattered—getting the astronauts home safely. As you will see in the following pages, God has a plan not only to rescue humans, but to fulfill His mission in the lives of rescued people. God's plan is designed to enable people to be fully alive.

We are fully alive when we live the best life we can live. It is a life where we have been forgiven of all our sins by God, been born again into a new life, and have entered into a life-long intimate relationship with Him. The new life begins when our sins are forgiven, and we become connected to God through the finished work of Jesus Christ. We literally have the life of Jesus living in us! Therefore, we live a joy-filled, righteous life where we play a role in advancing God's Kingdom throughout the earth. When we live life like this, we are *Fully Alive.*

ENDNOTES

1. From Academy Award-winning movie *Apollo 13;* Director: Ron Howard; starring Tom Hanks.

2. John H. Walton, The NIV Application Commentary: Genesis (Grand Rapids, MI: Zondervan, 2001), 130.

3. This obviously did not include the forbidden tree of the Knowledge of Good and Evil.

4. "The Fall" is the name that theologians have given to Adam and Eve's disobedience to God because it caused humankind's life and destiny to *Fall* drastically from God's original intent.

5. This has been the unfortunate condition of men and women to this day. Many women still seek to control men. In free countries, they may manipulate to get what they want. On the other hand, some men have held a violent upper hand, which has been devastating for women. For example in Muslim countries, under Shar'ia law, women are not considered to be equal to men. In many other places worldwide, women have been dominated by men in terrible ways including sexual violence.

CHAPTER TWO

God's Plan
has Not Changed

Renowned inventor Thomas Edison invented the first commercially usable light bulb. However, he did not get it right the first time he tried. In fact, he had many failures prior to getting it right. On one occasion he was asked why he kept trying when he had failed so many times. He replied, "I have not failed. I have just found 10,000 ways that won't work."[1] Armed with the knowledge that he had gained, Edison threw out what did not work, and kept trying.

God had created Adam and Eve with such hope. However, they failed miserably. We might think that God would give up on humans, and create another race of beings better equipped to carry the image of God in such a way that they would glorify Him and fulfill the lofty purposes of advancing His Kingdom throughout the earth. He is God. He can do anything He wants. He would certainly have been well within His rights to start over. However, unlike Edison who threw out what did not work, God determined that He would fulfill His mission with humans, the descendants of Adam and Eve.

We get our first glimpse of God's resolve to take His Kingdom to the ends of the earth through humans immediately after Adam and Eve's rebellious act of eating from the tree of good and evil. During God's first encounter with them, He told them the results of their disobedience. In the course of this conversation, God told Satan what would happen to him, as well. God told him that one of the woman's descendants would crush his head, even though Satan would crush His heal (Genesis 3:15). Many Bible scholars believe that this passage foreshadows Jesus totally defeating Satan, as He took the penalty for our sin on the cross (which is the flesh wound administered by Satan) and rose victoriously on the day of His resurrection.

Although this may seem like an obscure reference to God's desire to use humans, there are many clear references that point out His desire.

Noah's Commission

As the descendants of Adam and Eve became increasingly depraved, God expressed grief that He had made humankind, and said that He would destroy them. But a man named Noah caught God's eye. He was a righteous man, seeking to live as God had desired from the beginning, so God devised a plan to start over with Noah (Genesis 6:5-9). He instructed Noah to build a large boat in order to preserve Noah, his family, and two of every kind of animal (seven pairs of some animals) during a worldwide flood that would annihilate the rest of humanity and animal life. In this way, God brought judgment on humanity for the evil they had done, and provided an opportunity to start over. When the flood waters eventually receded and Noah, his family, and the animals left the ark, God told Noah, *"Be fruitful and increase in number and fill the earth"* (Genesis 9:1). God gave

Noah the same command that He had given to Adam and Eve. He still wanted to see His rule expand over the entire earth, and He still had great plans for humankind. He wanted men and women to experience the fullness of the image of God that He had placed within them, and to have the tremendous joy of fulfilling a great purpose.

Once Again, God has a Plan

The earth began to be populated once again. Some people began to move to the east and came upon a place called Shinar. They enjoyed being together, and decided that instead of being scattered throughout the earth, as God had intended, they would disobey Him, build a city and stay together. By doing this, the inhabitants of Shinar declared that they knew better than God what was best for them. They reasoned that life would be better if they would stay together. So, they built a city in defiance of God's command to be fruitful and multiply and fill the earth.

Once again, humankind exercised reasoning and decided to disobey God's clear command. This time, instead of destroying all of humankind or at least most of them, as He had done previously, He brought confusion to them, by giving them different languages, so they could not communicate with one another and escalate their rebellion (Genesis 11:1-9). Interestingly, when they could no longer communicate with one another, they scattered throughout the earth.

Again, God could have given up. He could have said, "I have tried two times and it appears humankind is so flawed and rebellious that the people will never get it right!" But God had made us in His image. He created us to be like Himself and to take the Kingdom to the ends to the earth. He knew our potential and He knew that we *could* get it right. He had a purpose for us and He was not going to give up.

Although God did not destroy the majority of humankind this time, He once again started over by calling a righteous man, Abram, whom He eventually renamed Abraham. God knew that Abram knew the voice of God and he would obey Him. On one occasion, the Lord spoke to Abram, telling him to leave the security of his family and go to a place He would show him later. Notice that Abram obeyed God even though he did not know where he was going, because he trusted in the wisdom and goodness of God. When God gave Abram this command to leave his home land, He also gave him a promise that he would be blessed and that, *"all peoples on earth will be blessed through you"* (Genesis 12:3).

God did not destroy the other inhabitants of the earth because He had determined that He would use Abram and his descendants to bless them, by showing them the greatness of God and His plan for humankind. Because Abram continued to obey God, He unfolded more of His plan, telling him that He would give him and his descendants a place to live (Genesis 15:7) and that he would become the father of many nations, with descendants as numerous as the stars in the sky (Genesis 17). He made a covenant with Abram and his descendants that would be good for generations.

A key part of the covenant was that God would enter into a relationship with them and teach them how to live as His children. God showed His commitment to keeping His part of the covenant by reaffirming it with Abram's son, Isaac, and his grandson, Jacob. Eventually, God clarified the way He desired them to live by giving them the Ten Commandments as the cornerstone of their relationship with God and with others.[2] God also let them know that He wanted the other nations of the world to observe how closely Israel walked with God so that they could see the great understanding and wisdom that comes from Him. His desire was that the peoples of the nations would become jealous of the life that Israel lived so that they would seek the God of Israel for themselves (Deuteronomy 4:5-8). In expressing this desire, God showed that He planned on reaching the nations of the world through a community of righteous people who walked so closely to God that their lives would cause others to pursue what Israel possessed.

Isaiah restates God's desire for Israel saying, *"I will also make you a light for the Gentiles, that my salvation may reach to the ends of the earth"* (Isaiah 49:6). Abram and his descendants, Israel, were destined to bring the "good news" of God's desire for His children to all the nations of the world. God had raised up Israel to be a people and a nation whom He sent into the world to show others that there is a God, a God of truth, who desires to know them and give them abundant life.

ISRAEL FALLS SHORT AGAIN

A cursory reading of the Old Testament reveals that Israel had moments when they walked in righteousness. There were great revivals under kings like Hezekiah, Josiah, and Joash, who so loved God and His Word that they led the entire nation to seek Him wholeheartedly. During these times, the citizens of other nations may have observed the closeness of Israel to her God. They may have observed the joy that came from living a life of holiness. Perhaps there were Gentiles[3] who wanted Israel's God. We know that this happened during the early reign of King Solomon, the son of King David.

As Solomon obeyed God and built the temple as a place for Israel to worship God, God blessed Solomon and Israel. Solomon exercised God-given wisdom and the nation experienced unparalleled blessing. All the nations around Israel began to hear about the greatness of Solomon and his wisdom. On one occasion, the queen of Sheba came to see the wealth of Israel and glean from the wisdom of Solomon. As she was leaving, she said that Solomon's wisdom was much better than his reputation (1 Kings 10:1-13). We also know that Babylonian King Nebuchadnezzar acknowledged Daniel's God as the one true

God when he came to his senses, after a period of insanity (Daniel 3-5), and Medeo-Persian King Darius (Daniel 6) praised Daniel's God after Daniel was thrown in a pit with hungry lions, and lived to tell about it.

Unfortunately, Israel's history confirmed that the human heart was evil continually (Genesis 6:5). As we read the Old Testament Book of Judges, we see the people of Israel going through times of national revival only to revert to evil. Each time Israel forsook the Lord, God raised up a judge who would lead them to a time of revival. However, the peak of each new revival was less righteous than the one before. Israel's downward turn, which took them deeper and deeper into depravity, was almost imperceptible. Eventually, in Judges 19, we discover an event occurring in Israel that was almost exactly like the famous events in Sodom and Gomorrah (Genesis 19). The only difference is that the sins committed by Israel (Judges 19) were averted in Sodom. The men of the city in Israel raped a man's concubine all night until she died from the ordeal.

Later in Israel's history, the nation asked for a king so they could be like other nations. They had abandoned their purpose to demonstrate the greatness of God to the nations to become like them. Samuel, the judge at the time, assumed that they had rejected him. However, God said that they had not rejected Samuel, but God Himself (1 Samuel 8:7). Many of these kings led Israel into idolatry and other kinds of sin. The wicked King Manasseh even sacrificed his children to the god Molech. As a result, God lowered the hedge of protection that He had provided for them when they walked in righteousness, and brought judgment upon them by using the armies of the Gentile nations. The Israelites, who lived through the battles, were relocated to other countries. As it was with Adam and Eve's banishment from the garden, God was exercising His severe mercy in order to call Israel to turn from their wickedness and seek the Lord. God knew that they would only fulfill His purpose if they repented of their idolatry and began to obey Him.

GOD'S ULTIMATE PLAN

Despite Israel's tendency to rebel against God, He still did not give up on them. He had a plan that would ultimately enable them to reflect the life of God and display to all humankind what God can do in the lives of His people. God spoke through His prophets not only about their current situation, but also about His plan for the future. In this chapter, we will look at the promises given to ancient Israel by God concerning the future.

God used Moses to lead the Jewish people out of Egypt and to prepare them to enter the Promised Land. During Moses' tenure as their leader, God gave Israel the Law, which laid out the principles designed to enable the people of Israel to live life to its fullest, and to provoke the Gentile nations to hunger for a relationship with Him that would also give them this same full life. As he was getting ready die, Moses told the Israelites that God would raise up another Prophet, like himself, who would speak the words of God. Throughout Israel's history, they looked for this Prophet, who would give them a "new law."

The people in Jesus' day continued to look for this Prophet who would empower them to fulfill God's plan. On one particular day in the life of Jesus, He had taught a group of people who had followed Him into the wilderness. They had not eaten, so He fed more than 5,000 people by miraculously multiplying one small lunch. After Jesus performed this miracle, which must have reminded them of Moses who fed the ancient peoples daily with manna from heaven, some concluded that Jesus was that Prophet, and they sought to make Him King (John 6:14).

The Old Testament Scriptures tell us that the second Prophet would be different from Moses. Isaiah tells us:

The Spirit of the Sovereign LORD is on me, because the LORD has anointed me to proclaim good news to the poor. He has sent me to bind up the brokenhearted, to proclaim freedom for the captives and release from darkness for the prisoners, to proclaim the year of the Lord's favor and the day of vengeance of our God, to comfort all who mourn, and provide for those who grieve in Zion—to bestow on them a crown of beauty instead of ashes, the oil of joy instead of mourning, and a garment of praise instead of a spirit of despair. They will be called oaks of righteousness, a planting of the LORD for the display of his splendor (Isaiah 61:1-3).

Isaiah tells us that the second Prophet will have the power to change the broken places in human lives so they will no longer be hindered by the emotional and spiritual problems that hinder them from fulfilling God's purpose. This second Prophet will not only proclaim truth, but when He teaches, lives will change.

Isaiah continues his discussion of the Prophet by telling his hearers that He will not only change lives, but He will use these changed people to rebuild cities (Isaiah 61:4) and receive a *"double portion in your land"* (Isaiah 61:7). The ministry of the Prophet will be so powerful that He will take broken people and develop them into the kind of people who will advance God's Kingdom in cities and throughout the world.

Let me explain why I believe this passage tells us that those changed by the Prophet will change the world. In ancient Israel, the firstborn son received a double portion of the inheritance. If there were two sons, the inheritance would be divided three ways and the older son would receive two portions. If there were five sons, the inheritance would be divided six ways and the older son would receive two portions. When Isaiah talked about the double portion, he meant that everyone ministered to by the Prophet would receive the inheritance of a firstborn son. I believe Isaiah is specifically talking about the firstborn Son, the Lord Jesus Christ.

As we look at Psalm 2, we find that the inheritance of the Son of God is the nations of the world. Therefore, when we receive the double portion in the land, we receive part of the Son of God's inheritance. We will touch nations. This is what God told Adam and Eve, Noah, and the nation of Israel that He created them to accomplish. This second Prophet will enable humans weakened by the Fall to be restored—so they will fulfill the purposes of God.

THE LAW INSIDE, NOT OUTSIDE

The Law had been given supernaturally as God spoke directly to Moses. God even inscribed the Ten Commandments on the stones Himself. Moses then presented the Law to Israel as their new way of life. However, because they had become separated from God's power at the Fall, they did not have the ability to obey these laws. They failed, even as Adam and Eve had. They took the Law, the spoken Word of God, filtered it through their corrupted reasoning, and decided which laws they would obey or not obey. They failed to obey the Law or they concocted regulations to assist them in obeying that were far from God's intent when He gave the Law. In many cases, they rejected the Law altogether and lived like the nations around them.

God had a better plan. He inspired Jeremiah the prophet to say, *"I will put my law in their minds and write it on their hearts"* (Jeremiah 31:33). In other words, God said: I will not engrave My law on stone, but rather on their hearts. The law of God will become an integral part of them, planted deep inside them. Therefore, they will obey the Word of God, spoken by the second Prophet. As they obey, their lives will attract others to follow Me.

God's promise of the Prophet shows His resolve to work in the lives of all people, to redeem them from their depravity and restore them to their creation purpose.

A KING IN THE LINE OF DAVID

God has shown His resolve to restore us to our calling through His command to Noah, through the call of Abraham, and His promise to bring a Prophet who would preach the Word of God and change lives through placing His law in our hearts. This would motivate the people of Israel to look to the day when God would fulfill this promise—as it should also motivate us today having received His promise of Jesus who lives within our hearts through the Holy Spirit.

There is one more promise that shows that God desired to restore Israel to His original plan. God told David that His covenant with him was everlasting. God promised David that he would always have a descendant upon his throne (2 Samuel 7:1-29; 23:5 and Ezekiel 37:24). A study of the history of Israel shows that there were times when David's descendants did not occupy the thrown of Israel. During some of that time, Israel was in exile. In fact, during the time of Jesus, Israel was in subjection to Rome. However, David and Israel believed that God would send One from David's lineage who would restore Israel to her rightful place, in order to communicate the heart of God to the world. As Israel studied the Scriptures, they concluded that God planned to send a future King. The people in Jesus' day believed that the King was also the Prophet. We understand this because those who concluded that Jesus was the Prophet, sought to make Him King (John 6:1-15).

Many years before the people tried to make Jesus King, God told Israel to prepare a spiritual highway that would facilitate the King's coming. God actually asked them to do this during one of Israel's darkest hours, saying, in essence, "Prepare for your King. He is coming. I have not forgotten My promise. Don't give up your hope, no matter how difficult times get. In fact, during this time, when things look so dark, prepare for the Lord's Messiah, the King and Prophet who will come to change the world." Isaiah said when

He comes, *"...the glory of the Lord will be revealed, and all people will see it together..."* (Isaiah 40:3-5).

My wife and I have seen a great illustration of how this spiritual highway will work. When we first started going to India, we traveled from Mumbai to Nashik. The road was two lanes and crowded with thousands of cars. We noticed, however, that they were working to widen the road to facilitate the growth in these cities. Each time we traveled between them, we noticed that more and more of the highway had been finished. They were preparing the way. Today, it is a toll road that makes the trip much easier. Isaiah was telling the people of Israel, if they got rid of the things that hinder God from working, it would be much easier for the King to come and do His work. We will talk more about this in chapter nine.

In Summary

God has not given up on humankind. He has consistently sought to reveal that He desires humankind to live in the way He created them to live. He has sought to communicate with humans through His chosen servants: Adam, Noah, Abraham and his descendants, Israel. Although God's plan seemed to have failed, He was preparing to unleash His ultimate plan. He gave glimpses of this plan throughout Israel's history, to instill hope that a day was coming when they would be rescued from the curse of the Fall, and be ushered once again into the Kingdom of the Messiah, the Kingdom of God. He would accomplish this through His Prophet-King who would teach the Word of God and place it upon the hearts of all people. His Kingdom people would demonstrate the glory of the Lord and men and women from every tongue, tribe, and nation would become part of that Kingdom. They would come to know Him, and they would give their lives to fulfill His purposes, to advance His Kingdom throughout the earth. God would fulfill His plan. He is God, and He will accomplish what He intended.

ENDNOTES

1. www.goodreads.com/author/quotes/3091287.Thomas_A_Edison; accessed 10/19/2013.

2. Of course there was much more to the Law of Moses laid out in Exodus through Deuteronomy, but the Ten Commandments give us the crux.

3. Non-Jewish people.

CHAPTER THREE

Jesus is the One Sent by God

Adam and Eve sought the ability to determine right from wrong, without the input of God. Humanity's desire for independence has had tragic results, which continue to impact us. In our quest to find life's meaning and describe the ideal life, we have come to many conflicting conclusions. We do not need to study them for very long before we conclude that they cannot all be true.

If we study economics, for instance, we find that communism and socialism believe that collective humanity administered by the government will solve not only economic, but social problems. Capitalism, on the other hand, tells us that individuals, with minimal interference from the government, will stimulate a robust economy and make society healthy. *These different economic systems can't all be correct.*

When it comes to religions, some tell us that all roads lead to heaven. However, a quick look at the major religions shows irreconcilable differences. Christianity, Islam, and Judaism all embrace one God. Judaism is the oldest of these religions and teaches that their God, Jehovah, has given them the Law of God, which instructs them how to live. They believe that the Prophet-King will come to place that law upon their hearts restoring them to the place where they will inspire the peoples of the world to worship Jehovah. However, they do not believe He has come yet.

Christianity also worships Jehovah, but its followers assert that Jesus Christ, the Prophet-King, has already come. Christians believe that Jesus' life showed believers how to live, and that His death and resurrection paid the penalty for sin. For those who believe and receive Him, He enters their lives, writes the truth of God on their hearts, and uses them to promote His message worldwide through righteous living and proclaiming His teaching.

Islam believes that Jesus, and many of the great men of Judaism, were prophets. However, they believe that Muhammad was the last, supreme prophet, who should be listened to because he gave the final revelation. Muslims do not believe that men are born in sin, as do both Judaism and Christianity, but rather that men and women sin because of their environment. Therefore, they seek to spread Islamic Law (known as Shar'ia) throughout the world. Muslims believe that when everyone in the world lives by Shar'ia, the world will have peace. They seek to win converts by sharing their message; but if nonbelievers do not respond to preaching, some Muslims believe they should force non-Muslims to convert or live under Shar'ia, which is the only hope for world peace.

Not every religion believes in one god. Hinduism and Animism believe in many gods and those embracing pantheism believe that everything is god. Our travels to India have shown us that although there are similarities in the various forms of Hindu, adherents do not all worship the same god. With 330 million gods, it would be impossible for them to worship them all. Some of the world's peoples do not believe in any god, or at least they cannot be sure there is a god. *These different beliefs and practices can't all be correct.*

So, who should we believe? This is the most important question anyone will ever ask because these divergent versions of "truth," cannot all be true. So we must ask, "Where can I go to find truth? Who can I depend on to lead me in the right direction? *Who truly is the Prophet of God?"*

The apostle John understood how important it is to go to the right source to discover truth. He spent the majority of his Gospel convincing his hearers that the One we should listen to is the Lord Jesus Christ. John records forty incidents, in twenty-one chapters where Jesus declared that He had been sent by God. Jesus understood that no one would take Him seriously, unless He could establish that *God had indeed sent Him.* If Jesus could establish that God had sent Him, then He had the authority to proclaim truth even if it meant making adjustments to long-standing religious practices. This became important because Jesus did not always conform to the practices instituted by the Jewish religious elite. For instance, the Jews had determined that no work, including healing, should take place on the Sabbath. However, Jesus violated this "law," at least the rules established by Judaism's religious elite, by healing on the Sabbath. Therefore, the religious leaders rejected Jesus' authority.

We see this after Jesus healed the man at the pool of Bethesda on the Sabbath (John 7:16).[2] "How can this man be from God if He does not keep the Sabbath?" they reasoned. On another occasion, Jesus took a whip and drove those who were selling animals for sacrifices out of the Temple. In the process, He overturned tables, making quite a scene. Because the leaders had authorized selling in the Temple area, they challenged Him and asked, *"What miraculous sign can you show us to prove your authority to do all this?"* (John 2:18; see

John 2:12-22). The Jews acknowledged that there would come One who would have authority to challenge and change their practices, but that person better be able to show a sign so amazing that they would know He was the One. Jesus told them that He would die and be resurrected. (We will discuss this in greater detail later.)

John had become convinced that Jesus had been sent from God. Therefore, he felt compelled to prove that Jesus had the right to speak for God.[3] (We will look into these proofs during the remainder of the chapter.)

MIRACULOUS SIGNS

When I am traveling, I depend upon signs. There are times when I miss a turn and exclaim that the turn was not well marked. Signs point to something. The Jews who confronted Jesus after He had chased those selling sacrifices out of the Temple, understood this. As a result, they demanded that Jesus show them a sign to validate His authority. Jesus also believed that miraculous signs served as proof that God had sent Him. When a group of "followers" rowed miles to see Him, He rebuked them by telling them that they only followed Him because He had fed them the day before, and not because of the signs.

If they had followed Him because a miraculous sign had convinced them that He was the Prophet-King, their desire to follow Him would persist in spite of difficulty because they would be convinced that He was the One. This was not the case because a few verses later, they all abandoned Him. Since Jesus' religious opponents made miraculous signs a test of Jesus' authority, we will begin our look at the proof of Jesus' claim of being sent by God by looking at the miraculous signs recorded by John. John said that he had chosen his material to enable us to believe in Jesus and have life in His Name (John 20:30-31). These miraculous signs fall into three categories: miracles of information; miracles over nature; and miraculous healings.

MIRACLES OF INFORMATION

As Jesus began His ministry, He looked for those who would learn from Him, follow Him, and eventually carry His message to the world after He went back to heaven. Early in that process, He met a man named Nathaniel. Although Jesus had never met Nathaniel, He immediately affirmed him as a man of integrity. Nathaniel never denied Jesus' assessment, but wondered how Jesus could know him, having never met him. Even though Jesus told him that He had seen him from a distance before Philip called him (John 1:44-51), there is no way that Jesus could have known about Nathaniel's character from a quick glance. We must conclude that God the Father had miraculously revealed this information to Jesus.

On another occasion, Jesus was chatting with a woman at a well where He sat to rest. As they began to talk of spiritual things, Jesus asked the woman to get her husband and bring him to the well. She explained that she did not have a husband. Jesus thanked her for her honesty and said you are right. You are now living with a man you have not married, and you have had five husbands. How could He know this? Even in the moral climate of twenty-first century America, no one would guess that someone had been married five times. The explanation: God told Jesus that this woman had been married five times. The woman showed that she understood this when she said, *"Sir...I can see that you are a prophet"* (John 4:19).

Jesus possessed information that came directly from His Father. If, God speaks directly to Jesus, then He must be the man of truth that we should listen to.

MIRACLES OVER NATURE

Turning Water into Wine. John tells us about a time when Jesus and the disciples had been invited to a wedding. The wedding went on for quite some time and the supply of wine ran low. It appeared that the family had not planned well. However, this might not have been the case. My wife and I have had the privilege of attending several weddings in India. Culturally, these weddings would be more like those in ancient Israel. Although there may be invitations for Indian weddings, anyone who hears about the wedding may attend. When someone attends the wedding, the family is expected to feed them. It would be embarrassing to run out of food, or in this case wine. Perhaps many more people attended this wedding than the family had anticipated. Whatever the reason, the wine was about to run out. Jesus' mother, knowing that Jesus knew how to handle difficult situations, told the servants to do whatever He said to do. He solved the problem by turning water into wine. Not only did He perform this miracle, but also the wine He miraculously created tasted better than the "best" wine served at the beginning of the celebration (John 2:1-11).

Feeding Five Thousand with One Small Lunch, and then Walking on Water. John recounts another situation where Jesus defied nature. After teaching for a long time, Jesus wanted to feed His guests. This was typical hospitality for that part of the world. His disciples did not how that would be possible. Jesus then took a small lunch donated by a young boy, and blessed it. He had His disciples distribute food to the crowd. Everyone ate as much as they wanted and the disciples gathered twelve baskets of leftovers. John tells us that about 5,000 men (plus women and children) ate that day.

After this exhausting day, Jesus told the disciples to get into a boat and head to the other side of the lake. He remained behind, went into the mountains, and spent time with His heavenly Father in order to replenish spiritually. After the disciples rowed about three miles in strong winds, Jesus walked on water and joined them in the middle of the lake. In one twenty-four hour period, Jesus overcame the laws of nature two times. This demonstrates that He has been sent by God and that we should listen to Him (John 6:1-24).

MIRACULOUS HEALINGS

No one likes to be sick or see a loved one sick, especially if the sickness is debilitating or life-threatening. John records a number of miraculous healings in His Gospel.

The Official's Son. Jesus had come back to Cana in Galilee, where He had turned the water into wine. A royal official whose son was ill, went to Jesus to ask Him to heal the boy. Jesus did not even go to the man's house, but sent him home, with the promise that his son would be well. As the man made his way home, his servants met him to tell him that he needn't bother Jesus anymore, because his son had been healed. When the official asked when the boy had become well, he discovered that it was the very hour that Jesus had declared him healed (John 4:43-50).

The Lame Man at the Pool. There was a pool in a town named Bethesda. Many sick people stayed near the pool because occasionally an angel would stir the waters of the pool, and the first person in the water would be healed. Imagine the hope, and yet hopelessness. What if the angel stirred the waters and you were second in the pool, or what if you had a debilitating illness or injury that made it impossible for you to get into the pool? As Jesus went to the pool, He met a man who was unable to walk for thirty-eight years. Jesus asked the man if he wanted to get well. Jesus knew the man wanted to get well or he would not have come to the pool. However, the man was not aware of any who had been healed, unless they had been the first ones in the pool. He also knew that he would never be that person. Jesus told the man to get up. The man got up, picked up the mat he had been resting on, and walked home for the first time in thirty-eight years (John 5:1-15). Hallelujah!

A Man Born Blind. Jesus' greatest healing may have occurred when He met a man who had been born blind. When Jesus met the man, He spit on the ground, made some mud, put it on the man's eyes, and told the man to wash in the Pool of Siloam. The man did exactly what Jesus told him to do, and went home seeing! This miracle had not been performed in a vacuum. Others testified that this man had been blind, but now he could see. These witnesses included some neighbors and his parents. Does a miracle like this prove that Jesus is the One sent from God? The man who had been blind declared that Jesus had to come from God, because God only listens to godly men. He said, *"Nobody has ever heard of opening the eyes of a man born blind"* (John 9:32). Later, when Jesus revealed to the man that He was the One, the man worshiped Him (John 9:1-41).

A Woman Unable to Bear Children. Jesus has not stopped performing miraculous signs to demonstrate that He is from God. My wife, Kerry, and I married thirty-seven years ago. Not long after we were married, we discovered that she was unable to bear children. This broke both of our hearts, but especially hers, because she felt she had been created to be a mom. We went to a well-known hospital where the doctor confirmed that she would not have children. The doctor suggested some medication that might help the situation, but we decided to have the church elders anoint and pray for her (James 5:14-16). About a year later, Kerry felt very sick and after going to the doctor, she found out that she was expecting our oldest daughter, Kristin! Nearly three years later our second daughter, Allison, came into our lives. We are grateful for the healing power of the One sent by God.

THE TESTIMONY OF JOHN THE BAPTIST

The Jewish leaders continually challenged Jesus' authority. After Jesus healed the man at Bethesda; the Jews persecuted Jesus because He healed on the Sabbath. Finally, when Jesus recognized that the Jews would not accept His testimony, He encouraged them to consider the testimony of John the Baptist, whose preaching they embraced, at least for a while (John 5:35). John the Baptist's testimony about himself was that he was not the Messiah, but that he was *"the voice of the one calling in the wilderness"* (John 1:23). John's whole ministry was to assist people to build the highway[4] to prepare the way of the King.

John the Baptist had made some amazing claims about Jesus. John, the apostle, records two separate occasions where John the Baptist called Jesus the Lamb of God. On one occasion, he said that He was *"the Lamb of God, who takes away the sin of the world!"* (John 1:29; see also John 1:36). In calling Jesus the Lamb of God, John the Baptist alludes to the lambs that were sacrificed to pay for the sins of Israel. Actually, on the Day of Atonement, the priests would select two lambs. The first lamb was sacrificed to pay the penalty for sin, and the second was released into the wilderness to symbolize the fact that God carried the shame of forgiven sins away from His people. John the Baptist indicates that Jesus would be the ultimate and final Sacrifice who would pay the penalty for sin and carry our shame away.

Later, John the Baptist reveals that he did not know that Jesus was the One by his own discernment or intuition. The first time John the Baptist declares Jesus to be the Lamb of God, he said that the only reason he knew that Jesus was the One, was because the Father had told him that the one upon whom the Spirit rested is the One. Matthew tells us that when Jesus was baptized, the Spirit of God came upon Him (John 1:33-34; Matthew 3:16-17). John the Baptist said that he knew that Jesus was the One because of the miracle of the Spirit coming upon Him in a visible way.

John's actions also indicate that he saw Jesus as the One who was to come. First, as a rabbi, John had gathered a group of disciples around him. However, as he began to point people to Jesus, some of his disciples followed Jesus. John was glad to see them follow Jesus.

After Jesus' baptism, John the Baptist's popularity began to wane. He was not bothered by this, however, because he understood that God had commissioned him to point others to Jesus, and that God had planned for Jesus to eclipse him. The Baptist's ministry consistently reflected his understanding of God's plan. He would not have pointed his disciples to Jesus if he had not known that Jesus was greater than himself (John 1:35-51). Later, when the Jewish leaders taunted the Baptist because his popularity was losing ground to Jesus, he told them that he was happy that many followed Jesus. He humbly declared, *"He must become greater; I must become less"* (John 3:30). Everything about the words and actions of John the Baptist tell us that Jesus is the One sent by God. John says, "Listen to Jesus!"

THE TESTIMONY OF THE SCRIPTURES

There is another key question that every God-seeker must answer. Do the Scriptures as a whole tell us that Jesus is the One sent by God? We have already seen that John's Gospel testifies that Jesus is the Sent One, but what do the rest of the Scriptures say?

In the previous chapter, you read how God has never given up on us. He has always desired that we experience the life He created us to live. He knew that we would never experience that life if we did not hear the truth from the One He would send. Therefore, He inspired the Old Testament writers to tell their readers that He would send a Prophet like Moses and a King like David. The Prophet-King would be like Moses and David, but much greater. Jesus highlighted this truth when He told the religious leaders, *"You study the Scriptures diligently because you think that in them you have eternal life. These are the Scriptures that testify about me"* (John 5:39).

Although many rejected Jesus' claims to be the One sent from God, some did recognize Him as the One promised in the Scriptures. Remember the woman who had the five husbands? As she discussed religious questions with Jesus that she could not understand, she said that they knew Messiah would come some day and answer all their questions. Jesus told her that He was the One. She believed Him and went to her village to tell the people about Him (John 4:25-26,39).

Another group who recognized that Jesus was the Prophet-King was the 5,000 who had been fed from the small lunch. They reasoned that no one but the coming King could perform such a miracle. Even though they did not understand the kind of Kingdom He would establish, they understood from the Scriptures that He was the One promised by God.

Although the other Gospel writers spend more time showing how Jesus fulfilled Old Testament promises, John highlighted several fulfilled promises demonstrating that Jesus is the One sent by God. John the Baptist quoted the first fulfilled Scripture surrounding the life of Jesus. When they asked John to tell them whether he was Messiah, he told them that he was not but rather *"...the voice of one calling in the wilderness, 'Make straight the way for the Lord'"* (John 1:23). The Jewish people believed that there would be one who would come prior to the coming of the Prophet-King who would prepare people's hearts to receive her Messiah. As we have already seen, John the Baptist pointed to Jesus as the One they should listen to and obey.

John also shows that Jesus' entry into Jerusalem, prior to His arrest and execution, had been predicted. As Jesus entered into Jerusalem, the people recognized Him as the King of Israel. The Old Testament Scriptures predicted both His exuberant welcome (Psalm 118:25-26) and the fact that He would enter Jerusalem riding on a donkey (Zechariah 9:9). This seemed to be the high point in Jesus' career, but as you most probably know, things turned south quickly.

First, we find that the majority of the people who had been looking for the coming of the Prophet-King or Messiah rejected Jesus. Even the religious leaders failed to recognize that He was the One. This undoubtedly caused others to reject Jesus. After all, didn't it stand to reason that when Messiah would come, everyone, especially the religious leaders would recognize and follow Him? They may have thought they could not follow One who had been rejected by their leaders who understood the Scriptures better than they did.

In order to show that Jesus could be and was the One sent by God, John reminds his readers that the Scriptures predicted that the Prophet-King would be rejected by many. Isaiah predicted that so many would reject the Messiah, that He exclaimed, *"Who has believed our message...?"* (Isaiah 53:1). Later, as John recorded the events of Jesus' execution, he quoted three prophecies that describe Jesus' crucifixion. John told us that some have already begun to question the validity of Jesus' ministry because they believed that the Messiah would live forever (John 12:34). John answered the detractors by reminding them how the Scriptures declare that the Prophet-King was destined to die a horrible death at the hands of His enemies.

John gave three Scriptures to make his point. During His crucifixion, Jesus hung naked. John tells us that the soldiers, who had been looking on, divided His clothing. After each soldier got his share of the clothing, one piece remained. The soldiers were about to tear the extra piece, but decided that it was too valuable to destroy. They gambled to see who would receive the last piece of Jesus' clothing. David described this event in detail in Psalm 22:18.

Because death by crucifixion could take many hours, soldiers often broke the legs of those being crucified in order to speed up the process. They planned to break the legs of Jesus and the other two who were being crucified alongside Him. They broke the legs of the two men, but when they came to Jesus, they found that He was already dead, so they pierced His side to make sure He really was dead. When they discovered that He had died, they did not break His legs. The Old Testament predicts both the piecing of Jesus' side, and the fact that His bones were not broken. (See Zechariah 12:10 and Psalm

34:20.) The Scriptures testify that Jesus is the One sent by God. We should listen to Him—and draw the ultimate conclusion.

POWER OVER DEATH

One day Jesus received word that his good friend, Lazarus, was sick. We would anticipate that Jesus would go to him as quickly as possible, in order to heal him. However, Jesus waited several days. By the time Jesus arrived, Lazarus had been dead for four days. Lazarus' sisters both told Jesus that if He had been there, Lazarus would not have died. Jesus, however, told His disciples that it was good that He was not there because they would now see the glory of God. Jesus went to the place where they had buried Lazarus, and asked the people to remove the stone covering the grave. Jesus prayed and then said, *"Lazarus, come out!"* (John 11:43).

Immediately, Lazarus, covered in burial cloths, came out of the grave. This miracle had such an impact that Jesus' enemies not only tried to kill Jesus, but also Lazarus. The fact that he was alive after being in the grave for four days proved beyond any doubt that Jesus was the Prophet-King. (For more details into this story see John 11.) We must point out that Lazarus was not the only person Jesus raised from the dead. He also healed a young man being carried to his final resting place (Luke 7:11-17) and the daughter of a synagogue ruler named Jairus (Luke 8:40-56). Who else but God's sent One would exercise such power that He would raise not one, but three people from the dead? There can be no question: Jesus is the One sent from God. We must listen to Him!

THE TESTIMONY OF THE FATHER

However, the single most important event proving that Jesus was sent by God, is the resurrection of Jesus. John describes the incident when Jesus cleared the Temple of those who were taking advantage of people who had entered Jerusalem for a festival. It seems that these money collectors were cheating people by refusing to accept the sacrifices the people had brought for worship, and were selling them approved animals at a very high price. Jesus turned over the tables of those taking the money, and forced them out of the Temple using a whip. The religious leaders were incensed by Jesus actions and asked Him to prove that He had authority to do this. Jesus told them, *"Destroy this temple, and I will raise it again in three days"* (John 2:19).

John points out that Jesus was not talking about the building, but His own body. He was predicting His death and subsequent resurrection. God the Father did raise Jesus from the dead. What greater testimony could there be that God sent Jesus! If the Father had not sent Jesus, He could have allowed Jesus' voice to be silenced when He died. If Jesus had not been raised, the Jews could have taken Jesus' body from the tomb, marched it down the streets of Jerusalem, and rightly declared, "This man is dead. He is not the Prophet-King." However, the Father raised Him. He is alive! His grave is empty!

The Father testified on Jesus' behalf in other ways as well. Jesus told His opponents that the work He had been sent to do testified that the Father had sent Him (John 5:36). In essence, He said, "Look at the miracles. Look at what happens day in and day out through My ministry. How do you explain this unless you agree that the hand of God is on Me? If the hand of God is upon Me, then you must conclude that 'the Father sent Me.'"

As Jesus was approaching the time of His crucifixion, He was, understandably, troubled in spirit. He went to God in prayer, asking Him to glorify His Father's name through His life. The Father responded in an audible voice from heaven, *"I have glorified it, and will glorify it again"* (John 12:28). The crowd that had gathered also heard the voice. Some said it was thunder, but others thought that they had heard the voice of an angel (John 11:29). This incident is an illustration of the Father in heaven giving clear testimony that He had sent Jesus to be the Prophet-King, and He wanted everyone to listen to Him.

AN IMPECCABLE LIFE TESTIMONY

In one of His intense conversations with the religious leaders, Jesus told them that they were the children of the devil and then gave them a challenge. He asked them to prove that He had sin in His life. I can certainly tell you that if I threw out that challenge to my enemies or my friends, they would probably be able to quickly come up with some sins of mine! Although they accused Jesus of being demon-possessed, they could not point to one specific sin. What a testimony![5] (John 8:42-47). Who, but the One sent by God, could give opponents this challenge without being able to name one sin? Jesus lived the purist and holiest life ever! He knew how to live life. He is the One to whom we should listen.

IN SUMMARY

As we seek to find and follow the One sent by God, let's consider who has a better resume than Jesus? John the Baptist, one of the most famous religious figures of Jesus' time wholeheartedly endorsed Him, saying Jesus is the One. He knew Jesus was the One sent by God because God had told him that the Holy Spirit would physically come upon and remain upon the One He sent. John the Baptist knew Jesus was the One!

In addition, Jesus lived a perfect life showing that He was sent by God. His detractors could not find one sin to accuse Him of— He claimed to be who He is, the Son of God. Not only did John the Baptist give testimony that Jesus is the One, but the Scriptures also testify that He is the One, because He fulfills Old Testament promise after promise. Besides all this, Jesus performed daily miracles revealing information only God could tell Him, and demonstrating He had power over nature and disease.

Overshadowing all these convincing proofs, *Jesus rose from the dead.* God would never raise an imposter from the dead so that he could continue to proclaim his deceptive philosophies. We must conclude that Jesus is who He claimed to be. He is the Prophet-King who came into the world, changed lives, and restored them to God's original purpose. Jesus was sent from God as the Prophet of Truth! All who seek the truth must conclude that Jesus is the Son of God—yesterday, today, and eternally.

ENDNOTES

1. See the miracle of the man at the pool in John 5 and the healing of the man born blind in John 9.

2. Although this discussion takes place in John chapter 7, it must be referring to the healing at the pool in John 5, because it is the last miracle recorded by John.

3. See John 1:12 and John 20:30-21. We will spend more time discussing these verses in future chapters.

4. This was a spiritual highway. Getting rid of the high places is getting rid of pride. Building up the low places is for those who see themselves less than God does. The last two places deal with our twisted, wicked places and the places where we are rough around the edges. When these are dealt with in an individual, community, or nation, it is much easier for the King to come.

5. The writer of Hebrews tells us that Jesus experienced temptation, but did not sin (Hebrews 4:15).

CHAPTER FOUR

Fully Alive

After Moses led Israel out of Egypt, they had to go through the wilderness in order to get to the Promised Land. Life in the wilderness got very difficult. It did not look like they would ever live the kind of life God had promised through Moses. In spite of the miracles that paved the way for them to leave Egypt and be saved from Pharaoh's army, they questioned whether God had brought them into the desert in order to kill them. They concluded that the life they lived in Egypt was as good as it gets, so they developed a plan to go back to Egypt where they at least had three "square" meals a day and the security of knowing what tomorrow would be like, even though they had been slaves in Egypt.

We must ask the same question. Is our present life as good as it gets? Is our world situation really as good as it gets? Jesus says, "No!" He told Nicodemus that he could actually see and experience the Kingdom of God (John 3:1-16). He told the woman He met at the Samaritan well that He could give her a life where she would *"never thirst"* (John 4:14) again. He offered Peter and the rest of the disciples a life that had eternal purpose. In this chapter we will briefly describe key characteristics of a life that is fully alive. We will discuss many of the topics addressed in this chapter in greater detail later in the book. However, it is important to address them here so that we get a glimpse of what it means to be fully alive.

I. When We are Fully Alive, We Walk in Intimacy with God.

In Chapter 1, we discovered that the first thing Adam and Eve lost when they disobeyed God was their intimate walk with Him. They ate from the forbidden tree because they wanted to discern right from wrong on their own, without outside input. They did not realize that they would lose the most precious gift God had given, a close relationship with Himself. This meant that man and woman no longer received God's help in decision-making or His perspective on life. As a result, humankind's understanding of truth became skewed. This has led to the terrible events we see in our world such as war, poverty, murder, and rape. It has led to the founding of religions that satisfy humankind's desire for worship, and philosophies that seek to explain life's meaning, but have actually led people away from the truth proclaimed by Jesus. They have led to widespread depression, even among children. They have led to life that at best falls short of God's ideal; and at worst, to depression, drugs, and violence.

When people believe in Jesus and begin their new lives in Christ, the first thing restored is their relationship with God. Jesus said, *"Now this is eternal life: that they may know you, the only true God, and Jesus Christ, whom you have sent"* (John 17:3). Life begins with restored connection with God. Peter, leader of the early Church, told us that the reason Jesus lived and died was *"to bring you to God"* (1 Peter 3:18). Let's see what intimacy with God looks like.

Intimacy with God begins with meeting Him. A few years ago, I bought my wife a book for Valentine's Day.[1] It was a book written by former Islamic terrorist, Kamal Saleem.[2] After she read the book, she began to pray that God would give her the opportunity to meet Kamal. Through a miraculous series of events, we both had the privilege to meet this godly man. Perhaps there is someone you would like to meet: a president or ruler of some other nation; a famous business person or military conqueror. You would consider it an honor to meet them. However, meeting one or all of these people pales in comparison to the privilege of meeting Jesus Christ, the Creator of the universe (John 1:1-3).

The life Jesus offers begins as we connect with God through salvation. We receive salvation, sometimes called being born again, by recognizing that we have sinned against God, and will never know Him unless those sins are forgiven. However, because of His great love, God sent Jesus Christ, the sinless One to die in our place and pay the penalty for our sin. When we recognize that His death on the cross is sufficient to pay the penalty for our sins, and we hunger to know Him and have our sins forgiven, we exercise faith in Him and what He has done by asking His forgiveness and inviting Him to come into our lives, giving us the new life He promised. At that moment, the wall between us and God is removed, and we start our new lives by coming into a relationship with Him.

When we walk in intimacy with God, our relationship with Him continues to grow. I met my wife on a blind date through a wonderful friend. I really liked her right away. Before long, I realized that I loved her. That was more than thirty-seven years ago. As we continue to share life together, I see aspects of her that I did not see before. She is like a diamond, and I get to see and enjoy more facets all the time. As I get to know her more, I am challenged by her godliness, boldness, and desire to serve the Lord. She continually enriches my life.

The same thing happens as we share life with Jesus. He told His disciples that His Father would love those who obey Him, and that He and His Father would make their home with them (John 14:21,23). As we get to know Jesus better, our lives will become more like the lives God planned for us at creation. We become more and more alive. John told his readers that he wrote the Gospel so that *"... by believing you may have life in his name"* (John 20:31). (We will talk about this in greater detail later.) However, let me say briefly at this time, that when we get to know His name, we are growing in our knowledge of Him and relationship to Him. As we discover new aspects of His character and person, our faith increases and our lives are enriched in new ways. We get the privilege of experiencing God and watching Him change our lives.

Intimacy with God focuses our worship in the right place. Humans have been created to worship. Most of the world's nearly 7 billion people worship a god. Even those who say they do not believe in a god, worship something. People worship someone or something when they look to "it" to meet their needs.

For instance, humanists worship humanity. Although later versions of the manifesto do not talk as much about humanism as religion, "The first manifesto, entitled simply *A Humanist Manifesto*, was written in 1933 primarily by Roy Wood Sellars and Raymond Bragg and was published with thirty-four signatories including philosopher John Dewey. Unlike the later ones, the first Manifesto talked of a new religion, and referred to Humanism as a religious movement to transcend and replace previous religions based on allegations of supernatural revelation."[3] So we see that even those who do not hold to religious or philosophical ideologies, engage in worship.

The last time the Pittsburgh Steelers played in the Super Bowl, my wife and I were speaking in Western Pennsylvania. One day when we went outside to walk and pray, as we walked the streets near the church, we saw numerous Steelers banners and paraphernalia. I said to Kerry that if someone arrived from another planet, they would assume that we worshiped the Steelers! (Some actually may!) Our cable television provides many stations dedicated to sports and sports stars. You can get more sports information than anyone (except a sportscaster) needs, twenty-four hours a day from multiple stations. We also find programs telling us the most recent gossip about our favorite movie and television stars.

This information overload is a worldwide phenomenon. When we travel to India, the newspapers dedicate many pages to the lives of Hollywood and Bollywood[4] stars. The Steelers have not won the Super Bowl in a long time, and movie stars let us down. Sports teams and superstars generally do little to change our lives, except allow us to escape for a few hours into their world until we return to the reality of our lives. Humanism seems to be failing miserably as our world becomes more and more dangerous and depraved. So these things are not the answer. Likewise, some people worship money or fame, pursuing them as gods to be worshiped. But money and the adulation that comes with fame are fleeting and do not satisfy.

As we clearly saw in the last chapter, Jesus is the One sent by God. Therefore, only when we worship Jesus do we worship the One who is worthy. All the others are imposters, promising something they cannot deliver. The God and Father of the Lord Jesus Christ is Creator and God! He is the only One worthy to be worshiped!

When we walk in intimacy with God, we recognize that He is the One True God and we desire to worship Him with our voice and our life, we discover *Who* we were made to worship!

2. When We are Fully Alive, We Become More Like Jesus.

I find it interesting that even those who deny that Jesus is the perfect Son of God and Savior of the world have a positive attitude about

Him. Muslims see Jesus as a prophet, the Messiah, and able to heal. Unfortunately, they do not see Him as the last and final Prophet. Hindus see Him as one of their millions of gods. We have seen a picture of Him alongside other gods on a wall in Mumbai. Some atheists see Him as a great moral teacher. We may wonder why. The answer is that His life and character were impeccable. Wouldn't it be great to be like Him?

As we study the Gospel of John, we see Jesus promising His followers that they can become like Him. On Jesus' last night before His arrest and crucifixion, He tells His disciples that when they obey God's commands, He would love them. He says, *"I have told you this so that my joy may be in you and that your joy may be complete"* (John 15:11). Joy transcends happiness. We experience happiness when something good happens: receiving a promotion, accepting a new job, buying a dream car or house, dating that certain someone. However, happiness flies away when we get fired or there is no second date. Joy goes much deeper. Gary Burge says that joy comes from the resurrection. Jesus has conquered sin and death. Jesus has conquered Satan. Jesus is alive. He has ascended to be with the Father and prays for us (Hebrews 7:25). In addition, because Jesus is now at the right hand of God, we can go before Him in prayer to ask Him to change any situation. Our circumstances may not look good, but Jesus is in control and He answers prayer in miraculous ways.[5]

We also experience joy because we will someday be with Jesus for eternity. Although things may be difficult, we can look forward to spending eternity with Him. On that same night of His betrayal, Jesus said that He was going back to His Father to prepare a place for us. Apostle Paul explains that knowing we will someday be with Him produces joy in the most difficult circumstances. He says, *"For our light and momentary troubles are achieving for us an eternal glory that far outweighs them all"* (2 Corinthians 4:17). We have joy because our life is right with God, and we will someday be with Him without all the troubles we experience in earth. We know that our efforts and perseverance will be well worth it.

Therefore, those who are fully alive possess an inner confidence that enables them to experience joy in the midst of great difficulty, a joy based on the victory Jesus Christ has already won. Joy is akin to peace. In the midst of tribulation, we can be at peace, an inner calm even when things are difficult (John 14:27).

Imagine joy in the midst of the good and not so good, and peace when it looks like things are falling apart all around us. When we live with joy and peace, we are more like Jesus. When we are like Jesus, our lives will speak to others who will want to know how we can have peace and joy in difficulty and live with such purpose. Jesus tells His disciples that when they live like this, their lives enlighten those around them concerning what life can be. Jesus confirms this when He exhorts His disciples to become *"children of light"* (John 12:36). John tells us that Jesus had life in Him, and that His light was the light of all.

If we, as His followers, become children of the light, our lives also enlighten others. Only His life can enlighten. This means that when we are born again by the Spirit of God, the life of Jesus lives in us. The more we obey, the more we become like Jesus, and the more effectively we enlighten others. Those who are fully alive become like Jesus in every way, including His character. Paul goes into greater detail when he says that if we are controlled by the Holy Spirit, we will exude *"love, joy, peace, patience, kindness, goodness, faithfulness, gentleness and self-control"* (Galatians 5:22-23). This is the character of Jesus manifested in and through us. When we are *fully alive,* we are becoming increasingly like Jesus Christ!

3. THOSE WHO ARE FULLY ALIVE GIVE THEMSELVES TO THE PURPOSES OF GOD.

A recent study found that those who retired at age 55 were more likely to die in the next ten years than those who worked until age 65.[6] Moolanomy.com says, referring to the study, "Without a purpose people tend to live shorter lives. This is simply because without purpose, they will not have motivation to live. Sounds a bit morbid, but it's true. When Dan Buettner discussed his research on centurions (those living to over the age of 100) as a TED[7] presentation, he found that they were all able to tell him exactly what their purpose was. Ironic? I doubt it."[8] God designed us to function with purpose. One of the first things that God did was to tell Adam and Eve that He wanted them to *be fruitful and multiply."* God asked Adam and Eve and those who come after them to bring the Kingdom of God beyond the Garden of Eden to the entire earth. Right from the start, humanity had a challenging purpose.

Jesus has restored His followers to that very purpose—to take His Kingdom to the ends of the earth. After His resurrection, Jesus spoke to His disciples telling them, *"As the Father has sent me, I am sending you"* (John 20:21; see also John 17:18). We have already seen that Jesus is the One sent by God to reveal the truth to all people so they can live life as God originally intended. Now we see Him sending His disciples in the same way that the Father had sent Him. In order for us to understand our purpose, we must understand what the Father sent Jesus to do.

Jesus came to live, die, and rise again for the salvation of the world. Someone may then ask, "How can we be sent like Jesus was?" He died on the cross for our sins, rose to give us new life, and ascended to be with the Father, so we can walk in His authority. In this regard, those who ask the question are right. John the Baptist made it clear that Jesus is *"the Lamb of God."* No other Lamb is needed. We are not sent in this way. Jesus has already completed that task. There can be no salvation apart from His finished work on the cross. He is the One and only Savior. However, Jesus fulfilled other ministry, which we can do with the help of His Spirit.

Jesus came to show us how to live. Apostle John told us, *"In him was life, and that life was the light of mankind"* (John 1:4).

John told his readers that Jesus possessed life, real life. No one was ever as alive as Jesus. Therefore, His life shows us how to live. As mentioned previously, the people of Jesus' day, as well as our own, had many theories concerning the best way to live. However, Jesus, the Creator, possessed life from eternity. When He became a man, He lived life perfectly. Therefore, those who observed the life of Jesus, and those of us who read about it, become enlightened about how to live life.

When we are born again, Jesus comes to live inside us and we become *"children of light."* Because we have been born again, with the life of Jesus residing in us by His indwelling Holy Spirit, we possess the potential to imitate His perfect life and show the world what real life is. Those who live fully for Jesus live life at a level that demonstrates real life to those around them. Peter was the leader of the band of apostles. He said, *"Live such good lives among the pagans that, though they accuse you of doing wrong, they may see your good deeds and glorify God on the day he visits us"* (1 Peter 2:12). Peter says that some of those who observe your life will decide to follow Jesus so that they, too, can be fully alive. We are sent to show others how to live!

Jesus came to preach the truth. One of the great themes of the Gospel of John is the subject of truth. The Greek word truth is *aletheia.* Rudolf Bultmann says that to the Greeks this word "denotes a reality that is firm, solid, binding, and hence, true."[9] John's Gospel also uses *logos* and *rhema,* two Greek words translated "word," which are synonymous with truth, because the written and spoken word of Jesus is truth. Truth is the group of principles that describe the way the universe works. When we talk about our physical universe, we discuss things like gravity and the amount of oxygen it takes for humans to live comfortably. The Bible reveals spiritual truth.

Spiritual truth tells us how to know and walk with God. It tells us the way God intends us to live life. Jesus knew that the people of the world did not understand truth. Because humankind wanted independence, many theories about life emerged, but those theories lead to an empty life. As a result, men and women continued to hunger for something, someone to provide joy and peace. Billions live like this today—continuing to hunger. Many people believe that they understand truth, but they are not satisfied. Their "truth" has not produced life, real life, the Life of Jesus. They need to hear the truth so they can experience the abundant life that Jesus provides. As disciples of Jesus Christ, we have been charged with the task of telling them. We have been sent to know, live, and proclaim the truth.

Jesus came to perform miraculous signs pointing to Him as the Sent One. The Jewish leaders recognized that the One sent by the Father would perform miracles that would authenticate His claim to be the One. As we saw in the last chapter, Jesus performed miracles that demonstrated His power over nature, sickness, and death. These piqued the interest of many people. Some rejected Jesus' claims that He was the One, but many believed and followed Him. Before, Jesus left the earth, He told His disciples, *"whoever believes in me will do the works I have been doing, and they will do even greater things than these"* (John 14:12). When Jesus said this, He made it clear that He intended His followers to perform miracles, by the power of the Holy Spirit, as He had done, in order that their claim to be sent by God would be authenticated. He even told them that they would do greater things than these. What could He mean by greater things? Some have suggested that this means that Jesus' followers would perform more miracles than Jesus because they would be in many more places than Jesus was able to go. Although Jesus did intend that they would perform miracles in many more places, He had more in mind when He talked about "greater works."

John records a conversation that Jesus had with a group that had been persecuting Him. He had just healed the man at the Pool of Bethesda. He told them that He would do greater things and proceeded to tell them that the Father had given Him the power to give life to the ones that He desires. He later says that the ones who will receive this life are the ones who believe in Him (John 5:16-24). The greater work, then, is seeing people move from *"death to life"* (John 5:24). The greater work is leading people into a relationship with Jesus Christ so that their sins are forgiven, and they, too, will meet the Father and possess the life of Jesus. No work could be greater than this. If we only seek to see miracles, we miss the point of the miracles, which is to point people to Jesus so they will move from *"death to life."* God sent us to lead people to Jesus Christ. He often uses miracles to authenticate the message we preach is truth.

Jesus was sent to multiply Himself. As stated earlier, Jesus not only came to proclaim truth in His lifetime, but to reproduce others who would proclaim truth when He was gone. This is why Jesus carefully selected those in whom He would invest His life. John tells us, *"Now while he was in Jerusalem at the Passover Festival, many people saw the* [miraculous] *signs he was performing and believed in his name. But Jesus would not entrust himself to them, for he knew all people"* (John 2:23-24). Although many believed in Jesus, He would not entrust (same Greek word translated "believe" earlier) Himself to them. In other words, Jesus was not just looking for a crowd. He was looking for those individuals who would follow Him, no matter what circumstances they might find themselves in, and seek to produce others who will do the same. The reason: many "sent ones" would travel to more places in every generation until they had advanced the Kingdom of God everywhere. We have been sent to produce other sent ones so His Kingdom will move forward until the end of time.

Jesus has given us a great purpose. We are to spread the truth about Him to others who will do the same until it has been successfully preached everywhere on earth.

4. THOSE WHO ARE FULLY ALIVE, WILL LIVE THEIR LIVES WITH OTHERS OF LIKE-MIND.

Matthew, Mark, Luke, and John wrote what we have come to know as the Gospels. The first three end by commanding the disciples to go into the world to proclaim truth. We have come to know this as the Great Commission. John also records Jesus sending His disciples into the world to proclaim the Gospel. However, John focuses on another command. Earlier, Jesus told His disciples that they would possess His joy if they obeyed His commands. He then tells them that His command is to *"Love each other as I have loved you"* (John 15:12). Jesus not only tells us to love, but He demonstrates how to love. Just prior to giving the command to love, Jesus washed the feet of His disciples. This was a job for only the lowliest of servants. None of the other disciples washed each others' feet because the task was beneath them. When Jesus washed their feet, He demonstrated that He wants us to give ourselves to one another, no matter what that might entail. Of course, Jesus not only washed their feet, but He died for them—and for us.

Jesus repeated this command to love one another on a number of occasions. Often He told them to love one another, especially concerning the impending persecution they would experience as they proclaimed the Gospel. Jesus knew that living as a sent one (an ambassador of the Kingdom of God), would not be easy for the disciples because many would oppose them. He told them to love each other, support one another, and do whatever it takes to assist each other to be effective in their ministry. There would be no room for isolation or competition.

When we love like this, we help each other walk in intimacy with God, fulfill our God-given purpose, and become more like Jesus. When we love like this and depend upon one another at this deep level, we develop lifelong, intimate relationships. My dad and his army buddies stayed in contact with each other decades after World

War II because they had entrusted their lives to each other, as they engaged in a "great" cause. Their war experience bonded them for life. We serve in the "greatest" cause ever given to humankind. God has placed people around us who we can encourage and serve and who will encourage and serve us. What a privilege!

In Summary

Jesus Christ offers us the greatest life possible—we have the opportunity to get to know the living God intimately. Not only do we get to know Him, but we have the very life of His Son, the Lord Jesus Christ, living in us and giving us the potential to become increasingly more like Him. He also gives us the chance to become passionate about seeing multitudes of others enter this relationship and join us in this great task.

He has not sent us alone. He has given us others who will love, encourage, challenge, and partner with us, as we seek to expand His Kingdom throughout the earth, so that the world may become increasingly more like He intended it to be.

Unfortunately, God had revealed His great plan to others in the past and they failed. Why would He think things would go any better this time? In the next chapter, we will discover the reasons why things will go differently, this time. We will see why men and women will grasp the life God offers and walk it out.

ENDNOTES

1. I know, it seems strange to buy a book for your wife on Valentine's Day, but my wife and I are burdened for the world's Muslims and love to learn all we can about reaching them. She actually loved the gift!

2. Not his real name. It is the name he uses to protect those dear to him. You can read his story in *The Blood of Lambs* by Kamal Saleem (Howard Books, a division of Simon and Schuster, New York, 2009).

3. Wikipedia, "Humanist Manifesto"; accessed 12/4/2013.

4. Bollywood is India's version of Hollywood. It resides primarily in Mumbai. Bollywood produces more movies than Hollywood. If you are really into this, Pakistan's version is Lollywood, housed in Lahore.

5. Gary M. Burge, The NIV Application Commentary, John (Grand Rapids, MI, Zondervan Publishing House, 2000), 442.

6. Daniel J. DeNoon, WebMd, "Early Retirement, Early Death" article dated October 20, 2005; accessed 12/6/2013.

7. TED is an organization that spreads ideas in short teachings. TED stands for Technology, Entertainment, and Design.

8. www.moolanomy.com; "How to Die Young: Retire Early"; accessed 12/6/2013.

9. Gerhard Kittel and Gerhard Friedrich, eds., Theological Dictionary of The New Testament (Grand Rapids, MI: Eerdmans Publishing Co., 1985), translated and abridged by Geoffrey W. Bromiley. Article by Rudolf Bultmann, 37.

CHAPTER FIVE

What Makes You Think...

So what makes me think things will be better this time? Keep reading and you will find out.

The quartz watch was invented in Neuchâtel, Switzerland, in 1967. Unfortunately, the Swiss did not see a reason to develop quartz watches because they controlled the world market, making the best watches in the world. The rest of the world began to develop and sell quartz watches, and the Swiss share of the market dropped drastically. They did not see that the world was changing, and that this discovery could solidify Swiss control of the watch market. They continued to do what they had been doing with devastating results.

This reminds me of a church I heard about. The congregation had worked hard during the year seeking to win people to Christ. In fact, the church members had visited 1,000 homes, but with no tangible results. Someone asked, "What will you be doing next year to win the lost?" They replied, "We will visit 2,000 homes!" It seems amazing that no one asked whether the same ineffective method would yield better results if they just did more of the same. Wouldn't a new approach be better?

God sent His Son to preach truth to His people, but why would God think things would work out better this time? He had tried time and again to inspire His people to live for Him, and to fulfill His plan to reach the world. We have already discussed how Adam and Eve failed to follow God's plan. Later, when God started over with Noah and his family, we saw that those who followed Noah also failed.

The history of Israel, written in the Old Testament, outlines generations of God's people falling short of His original plan. Even after God miraculously delivered the Jewish people from slavery in Egypt, they became discouraged, worshiped the god, Baal, and planned to go back to Egypt. Fortunately, God stopped them.

Finally, after 40 years and the death of everyone who had been born in Egypt, God led the Jewish people into the land He had promised them. The writer of the Book of Judges tells us that after the elders who had served with Joshua died, the people began to practice evil in God's eyes and worshiped another god (Judges 2:10-11). As we read through the Book of Judges, we find at least nine times when Israel drifted so far from God that He brought judgment on them. When Israel repented and prayed, God mercifully restored them.

One of my Old Testament professors in seminary pointed out that although Israel came back to God these nine times, their "new" righteousness fell short of the righteousness they displayed the previous time they experienced revival. He said that the Book of Judges shows Israel spiraling downward during the period of the Judges. Israel came back to God, just not as far as they had been before their last fall. Slowly, almost imperceptibly, Israel became less and less like God desired them to be, until one of their cities sunk to such depravity that we are shocked by their sin. The sinful event looked like the events that occurred in Sodom centuries before (Genesis 19).

Unfortunately, the atrocities committed by Israel exceeded those in Sodom (Judges 19). We are shocked by the depravity because we did not see Israel's subtle decline. Once again, God's experiment to develop a holy people who would draw the nations of the world into His Kingdom, seems to have failed.

During the era of the Judges, the Israelites asked God to give her a king so she could be like the other nations (1 Samuel 8:5). Instead of possessing a relationship with God that would stir other nations to desire to know the God of Israel, Israel decided that she wanted to be like the other nations. God told Samuel, *"it is not you they have rejected, but they have rejected me as their king"* (1 Samuel 8:7). Israel had not only drifted in her morality and her walk with God, but now she rejected Him as her King.

To be sure, the Israelites had some good days. They came out of Egypt by the mighty hand of God, and were sustained miraculously for forty years in the desert. They defeated the Canaanites and took possession of the land that God had promised under the leadership of Joshua. They experienced revival many times under the judges and kings, like David, Solomon, Hezekiah, Joash, and Josiah. Additionally, government leaders like Daniel and Nehemiah had an impact upon pagan nations, and they helped change Israel's course, at least for a time.

However, even though a number of kings sparked national revival, the period of the kings was not, generally, a time when Israel fulfilled her God-ordained destiny. During the reign of the kings, Israel fell away from God on numerous occasions, as she had in the period of the judges. God mercifully sent prophets to call them to repentance, but in most cases, the people rejected the prophet and his message and continued to walk in sin. Finally, Israel's sin got so bad and lasted so long that God sent Israel into exile in Babylon. It is important to note that God did not judge them to destroy them in anger. On the contrary, God brought judgment upon Israel to get her attention, with the goal of sparking the kind of revival that would put them on the path He had planned for them since their inception. God is merciful and He continues to call His people to repent (turn back to Him) and return to His perfect, never-changing plan.

Even after the Babylonian exile, God gave His people another chance. He raised up Ezra and Nehemiah to bring the people of Israel back to the Promised Land and give them another chance to function as His ambassadors to the nations of the world. Besides rebuilding the Temple of God in Jerusalem, and rebuilding the walls of Jerusalem, these two men oversaw two great revivals. But by the time Jesus Christ came on the scene, the Jewish religious leaders, who had memorized the Scriptures that promised the coming of the Prophet-King, failed to recognize that Jesus was the One sent by God.

So, after thousands of years of starting over, why would God expect that things would be different this time? Let's see why.

Moses versus Jesus

"For the law was given through Moses; grace and truth came through Jesus Christ" (John 1:17). In this passage, John tells us that God revealed the Law (recorded for us in the Old Testament Books of Exodus through Deuteronomy) through Moses. As we read the Old Testament, we find the Law of Moses giving instructions for every aspect Israel's life: her relationship with God; her social interaction, including marriage and sexual intimacy; and her medicine and sanitation. There was little left to chance, and yet Israel failed to be all that God desired.

At this time, I need to answer a question that you may have. As we look at the failure of God's people throughout the Old Testament era, we might conclude that the Law itself is flawed. Paul, the New Testament apostle, answers this question for us as he reveals his own struggle to live righteously. He concludes that the Law is not at fault.

He says, *"So then, the law is holy, and the commandment is holy, righteous and good"* (Romans 7:12). Paul explains that we are the real problem. *"For sin, seizing the opportunity afforded by the commandment, deceived me, and through the commandment put me to death"* (Romans 7:11). Paul explains that he did not have the ability within himself to do the right thing. He concludes that the sin nature, which has infected every human since the sin of Adam and Eve, is at fault, because its nature is to rebel against God (see Romans 5:12 for an explanation).

When Adam and Eve sinned, they not only lost God's perspective on life, but acquired a nature that opposed God. In other words, the sin nature naturally rebels against God and His commands. Unfortunately, Adam and Eve passed this rebellious nature on to each succeeding generation. This is why Israel failed, and why humans everywhere have struggled to do what is right. If you have ever made a New Year's resolution, you know the battle that you face when you try to do what is right. We may have some successes, but apart from Christ, we find that our overall grade is not very good.

We can see a spiral downward as we look at the American culture. Although some will argue this point, the United States was founded on Judeo-Christian principles derived from the Old and New Testaments. However, we must admit that the moral fabric of America has been steadily declining for decades, if not centuries. Church attendance has declined, and with it, an alarming decline in biblical standards and ethics. What was scandalous a generation ago, has become the norm. Because our flesh rebels against God and His standards, culture naturally moves away from what God desires. Therefore, those who seek to police what is right and wrong, the Political Correctness (PC) gurus, have declared everything other than biblical, God-ordained values, to be acceptable. They want everyone to be tolerant of every lifestyle, regardless of what the Bible tells us. In fact, they have decided that Christianity—which dares to proclaim what

God says is right and wrong—is wrong. We have come to that point where we call what is right, wrong and what is wrong, right.

Israel, and all humankind apart from Christ, cannot keep the Law of God even if they have it written out and sitting on their shelf.

WHAT IS DIFFERENT ABOUT JESUS?

John tells us that although the Law came through Moses, *"grace and truth"* came through Jesus Christ. Truth describes life as God intended it. God's truth is not significantly different from the Law. The Law required Israel, and the people of Israel, to bring animal sacrifices to atone for their sin. The Scriptures tell us that Jesus obliterated the need for the sacrificial system, because He died for our sins as the final and eternally sufficient sacrifice (Hebrews 9:11-14). We also note that Jesus overruled some of the eating and sanitation laws.[2] However, the religious and moral laws remain essentially the same. For example, God still desires that His people keep the Ten Commandments, which actually summarizes the Law for us.

Jesus goes beyond merely giving the truth. He has provided the ability to live the truth to those who exercise faith in Him. Let's take a look at the various aspects of His provision, which we will call His grace during the remainder of this book.

I. JESUS HAS TAKEN AWAY OUR SHAME.

In Chapter 1 of this book, we talked about the decline of humanity after disobeying God. Immediately, Adam and Eve made clothes for themselves and hid from God, because they had become ashamed. They recognized that something was wrong with them, and they felt embarrassment about it. This caused them to hide from the only One who could solve their problem. Shame causes people to have low self-esteem. It may cause a person to engage in activities that are inappropriate, because they don't believe their life has enough value to wait for what is good. These inappropriate activities are sin, which means missing the mark of God's best for their lives.

Jesus is the Lamb of God. The difference with this Lamb is that His sacrifice was sufficient for all time. His sacrifice paid for humankind's sins—past, present, and future. Those who receive Christ's forgiveness not only receive forgiveness for past sins, but for all time. This means that they have been given a clean slate with new potential. Their past failures no longer need to define who they will be in the future. No matter what may have happened in their past, believers in Jesus can become new persons, because their conscience is clean. They can look at themselves with a new perspective, the perspective of God.

You may ask, "How can I receive forgiveness for my sins and a clean slate?" First, you must recognize that you have sinned and will continue to do so, unless you get some help. Second, you must recognize that in spite of your sin and failure, God loves you and has sent His Son, Jesus Christ to pay the penalty for your sin on the cross, and raised Him from the dead to make it possible for you to have a new life.

When you know that steps one and two are true, you will exercise faith that Jesus will forgive your sins and give you a new life. We show our faith by praying a prayer like this: "Jesus, I have sinned and messed up my life. I want to turn my life over to You, asking You to forgive my sins and come into my life and make me a new person." If you have never received Him, you can pray a prayer like this one. The words don't save you, but rather your heart that says, "I'm sorry and want to be forgiven, Jesus, and I want to live like You want me to live." Any person who does that will receive forgiveness of sin and become a new person with all the potential that we discussed in Chapter 4. In future chapters we will discuss the kind of life that will make us like God desires us to be. Praise God, He takes away our shame!

2. Jesus Has Given Us His Word.

We live in a confusing world. Many people may be giving conflicting advice on how to cope with life. As we have already seen, Jesus is the only One we can trust. He is the One sent by God. Humankind has become so confused that we assume that right things are wrong, and vise versa. Some of the world's religious leaders believe that the most righteous thing they can do is oppose the preaching of Jesus Christ. Even in the United States, founded upon biblical principles, the PC police tell us that it is not appropriate to wear a cross to work because it might offend someone, and that we should not call the Christmas Season, Christmas, but Winter Holidays.

They oppose biblical Christianity because it proclaims that some behaviors are forbidden and their desire is to give license to every lifestyle. God does not forbid certain activities because He is the eternal "spoil-sport" who wants to make life miserable. No. He wants us to make our lives as wonderful as possible by avoiding certain activities that will harm us. Sin is missing the mark. When we violate the truth, God knows that our lives will be less than He intended, so He tells us to avoid those things. His motivation is love. He wants us to be fully alive knowing that some activities keep us from that life.

I mention all of this because humankind has lost the ability to discern truth. We are headed down a slippery slope from which we will not emerge, by our own efforts. We will only understand truth if God reveals it to us.

In spite of humankind's penchant to disobey God, God has never changed His plan. When Adam and Eve hid from God, He sought them out and began to communicate with them immediately. Although God told Adam and Eve the consequences of their sin, He also told them of the coming of Jesus Christ during that first conversation. He told the snake, Satan, *"And I will put enmity between you and the woman, and between your offspring and hers; he will crush your head, and you will strike his heel"* (Genesis 3:15). God was telling Satan that someday he would give a flesh wound to the One who will crush him. When God talked about the flesh wound to the descendant of Eve, He meant the wound that Satan would give Jesus on the cross. When Jesus rose from the dead, He crushed the head of Satan, which makes it possible to release humans from the bondage of the sin nature and release them to live the life God has always intended. Although Adam and Eve probably did not understood what God meant, I believe Satan knew what God meant. God also said these things so that those of us who would live after Jesus would see that God's plan for us has never changed, even after the first tragic sin.

God has never stopped telling people that their lives can be different, fulfilling, and alive. He communicated with Adam and Eve. He communicated with and through the nation of Israel as He gave her the Law and as He spoke through the prophets. When humans could not live life as God intended, He sent the Promised One to them who would enable them to change. One of Jesus' names is "the Word" (Greek: *Logos)*. Jesus was and is God. He is Truth. When He lived on earth, He communicated truth through His perfect life.

After Jesus went back to be with the Father, the Holy Spirit inspired four men to write down what they had seen of the life and ministry of Jesus. The Holy Spirit, the third person of the Godhead, inspired these men to write so that there would be a God-inspired version of the life of the Prophet-Messiah-Son of God-Savior.[3] In addition, the Holy Spirit inspired a doctor named Luke to write a partial history of the early Church (the Book of Acts) to testify of the wonderful acts of the Holy Spirit through the early Church. He led men like Peter, Paul, and others to write inspired letters to encourage the fledgling Church and help correct problems that would have shipwrecked them. The Gospels, the Acts, and the Letters make up our New Testament, which completes the story of how God purchased salvation for all.

God communicates to us through the Old and New Testaments, and through the life of Jesus. Jesus tells the Father in prayer, *"your word is truth"* (John 17:17). The written Word of God supplies grace for us to succeed. Even though we cannot come up with truth on our own, He communicates it to us through His inspired Word. Let's take a look at some of ways that the Word of God enables us to live as God desires.

The Word of God is alive! (John 6:63; see also Hebrews 4:12.) Jesus tells us that *"...The words I have spoken to you—they are full of the Spirit and life"* (John 6:63). As humans, we need life. When the first humans sinned they became separated from God, which means they died spiritually. Unfortunately, this separation from God has been passed down to all humankind. When we became separated from God, the Bible tells us that our nature was to rebel against God, that is to sin. We call this tendency the sin nature. The only thing that can correct this situation is to move from death to life. This is exactly what happens when a person comes to Christ.

However, we still might ask, "Humankind has had the Word of God since the garden. What will make a difference this time?" Jesus gave the answer in a conversation He had with a religious leader named Nicodemus. He says that someone must be born again. We may wonder, as did Nicodemus, *How can this happen?* Jesus says that when someone receives Him, the person is born again; the moment a person asks Jesus Christ to come into his or her life, the Holy Spirit comes to live within that person. The part of us that died when Adam and Eve sinned comes alive.

Jesus tells us that the first change that takes place in a new believer's life is to see the Kingdom of God (see John 3:3-5 and Romans 8:9). New believers will see beyond what is seen with their natural eyes and mind. They will see all the spiritual realities not seen before, because now they are fully alive. New believers develop a type of sixth sense—perceiving the universe more completely.

At that point, the Word of God becomes more than words on a page, because the Holy Spirit takes the Word that believers hear and read, and gives them understanding that becomes part of their lives. When a person receives this level of understanding, it is called revelation. Revelation does not mean that God is giving new truth. He is not writing new books of the Bible, but rather, the Holy Spirit takes the truths of the Word of God and gives us understanding making them part of us. His Word becomes part of us, because it is in our heart (Jeremiah 31:33). This causes our actions to change. What grace!

The Word of God speaks of Jesus. After Jesus healed the man at the Pool of Bethesda, some Jewish leaders challenged Jesus because He healed the man on the Sabbath, telling the man to carry his mat. According to these leaders' interpretation of the Law, no work, including healing and carrying your mat, should be done on the Sabbath. How could Jesus be spiritual and do the work of healing on the Sabbath, especially when He told the man to carry his mat, they asked each other. As the discussion continued, Jesus applauded them for diligently studying the Scriptures, but He told them that they had missed the point because the Scriptures talk about Him (John 5:39). He told them that if they really understood the Scriptures, they would see Him and embrace Him as the Prophet-King. In other words, these religious leaders had studied and memorized the Scripture seeking to live the life of God, yet they missed the most important truth. They had not received revelation. Unless we receive revelation from God, we, too, will miss the point of Scripture and fail to live the life God intends for us to live.

Jesus knew how important it was for these leaders (and for us) to get to know Him through the Word of God. In fact, John tells us that the reason he wrote the Gospel was *"...that you may believe that Jesus is the Messiah, the Son of God, and that by believing you may have life in his name"* (John 20:31). When people believe that Jesus is the Christ, the Son of God, they will enter into a relationship with Him by being born again. John, however, wanted to see people go beyond that initial relationship with God, because he knew that real life comes from gaining a revelation of how amazing Jesus truly is. Only then would they be fully alive. As a result, John spends a great deal of time in his Gospel telling his readers who Jesus is. He wants them to gain a revelation of Jesus, and experience life in His name. Whenever we see the phrase "Name of God" or "Name of Jesus" mentioned in Scripture, it means that someone has received a revelation of who God is so powerfully that it is engraved in the man or woman's heart—and that person will never be the same.

For example, God had asked Abraham to sacrifice his only son. Abraham was immediately willing to obey. However, prior to killing his son, God provided a ram for the sacrifice, instead of Isaac. Abraham recognized that God is our Provider (Genesis 22). He was so changed that he would never doubt God's ability to provide for him.

I mentioned earlier that God healed my wife, which enabled her to give birth to our two daughters. This wonderful miracle has been planted on her heart. She loves to pray for couples who are unable to have children, and has seen a number of miracle babies born because of her faith in God's power to heal. She received a revelation of God as Healer (Jehovah Rophe) and was changed forever.

As we seek to know God, the Holy Spirit will continually give us revelation of the nature and wonder of the Father, Son, and Holy Spirit that we had not grasped before. As the Holy Spirit gives us this revelation, our faith is energized and we begin to live like God intends.

The Word of God sets us free. Jesus said, *"If you hold to my teaching, you are really my disciples. Then you will know the truth, and the truth will set you free"* (John 8:31-32). Jesus communicated a couple of principles when He declared these words. He made it clear that a believer is not truly His disciple if he or she does not obey His Word. How could we call ourselves followers of Jesus if we do not do what

He says to do? He also told us that we really only understand the truth when we obey it. We may wonder why we must obey the truth in order to understand it. The reason is that we really don't understand something completely until we experience it. For instance, I believe the Bible is the written Word of God. Therefore, I believe that God is the Provider. However, as I obeyed God by giving tithes and offerings,[4] and obeying Him by following Him into a faith ministry that, in the natural is financially risky, I experienced the provision of God.

My wife and I had two young children when I entered seminary. A family of four needs more money than the part-time job I had as a student. We often had little money left for food, and we did not receive sufficient salary to even place my seminary tuition in the budget. We told the Lord that He had led us to seminary and we would trust Him to care for our needs, including tuition, if He wanted me to complete my training. We ate three meals a day, and even snacks—praising the Lord for His provision. God also provided a couple of special vacations, supplied our daughters with bikes and a swing set, paid for a major car repair, paid all of my tuition on time for three and one-half years, and other miracles—without borrowing a penny.

We learn more by experiencing the Provider than by just knowing He provides intellectually. As we trust the Lord, He will prove Himself faithful; and His faithfulness will not only impact us, but provide testimony to others. During a seven-year period, at least one of our girls was attending a Christian college, and both of our daughters got married during that same period. God met our needs, every time. One incident stands out. Our older daughter, Kristin, was signing up for her last semester of classes. We needed to pay for her previous semester before she could register.

At the same time, our younger daughter, Allison, needed to pay her fall semester bill. The total due was $3,000, which we did not have.

Allison said, "I know God will provide," because she knew Jesus and had seen Him provide even things like bikes and swings; she had been touched by God our Provider. About the same time Kristin was going to pay her bill, Allison and Kerry went to the mail box to discover a strange letter. It was addressed to "Pastor John and Mrs. Kerry." Inside was a cashier's check for $3,000! We do not know who gave this money, except that God had inspired someone to bless us. This testimony has continued to encourage many people as we have shared it. As mentioned previously, we really get to know the Word of God when we personally experience it.

Jesus says that when you know the truth, it will set you free. After He makes this statement, Jesus tells His hearers that when we sin, we are slaves to sin. We must conclude that Jesus was telling His listeners that the Word of God delivers us from the slavery of our sin and sin nature, setting us free to be new people. We have seen the Kingdom, and therefore we have a new perspective. Jesus says that He not only wants us to see the Kingdom, but enter it (John 3:5). We get this new perspective when the Holy Spirit highlights the Scripture's meaning, and then empowers us to obey the Word. Instead of missing the mark, we begin to hit the bull's eye of life in God. Hallelujah!

The Word of God protects us from the world. Just prior to telling us that God's Word is truth, Jesus prayed that God would *"Sanctify them by the truth"* (John 17:17). The word "sanctify" means to set something apart. Some women have special dishes that they set apart for important occasions. They are not used for anything else. When Jesus asked God to sanctify His disciples, He asked Him to set them apart from the world. The world consists of all the religions and philosophical perspectives that have been "discovered" by humans, as they have sought to understand right from wrong. These perspectives have forged the way that men and women think. It is obvious that the religions, philosophies, lifestyles, and cultures that people have developed have not solved individual or corporate problems. In fact, they have made the problems worse.

Jesus prayed that His followers would become so immersed in His Word that the revelation they receive would deter them from following the futile thinking of worldly schemes and the problems they produce, and be set aside for God's Kingdom purpose. He is saying, "I don't want them wasting their time on what doesn't satisfy, but on what gives Kingdom life." The Word of God gives us God's perspective on life. It sheds light on the deficiencies of the world's thinking and elevates us to Kingdom thinking. As a result, we stay away from the things that will ruin our lives and dedicate ourselves to living the life God has offered us. The Word of God helps us to be fully alive.

3. God Gave Us the Holy Spirit.

We have already discussed how the Holy Spirit takes the written Word of God and makes it so real to us that our behavior changes. However, this is not the only role that the Holy Spirit plays in enabling us to live the way the Father desires us to live. Although there are many more, let's consider the following three ways the Holy Spirit helps us through life.

The Holy Spirit makes us alive. When Adam and Eve disobeyed God, they and their descendants died spiritually. They still looked very much alive—their minds, bodies, and emotions continued to function—but God's Spirit withdrew from their human spirit. In this state, they still accomplished much including the development of agriculture and manufacturing, music, and city-building (Genesis 4:20-23 and Genesis 11). However, all was not well. We know that Cain killed his brother, Abel. Later, Lamech killed a man who stood in the way of what he wanted. Lamech's murder is recorded after the author of Genesis tells us about the agricultural, manufacturing, and musical advances. Humankind continues to make technological and cultural advances, with breakthroughs in air and space travel and communications, including smart phones and the Internet.

Recently a friend came from Pakistan to the United States. His wife wanted him to bring her a coat from America. Late on a Friday evening, Kerry tried on coats and then took photos and sent them to his wife in Islamabad, via text messaging. She would express her opinion within seconds, and eventually chose the coat she wanted, even though she was 9,000 miles away! Humankind's great advances, however, have not stopped people from murdering each other or instigating national tensions throughout the world. In fact, they may have intensified them because now we have more sophisticated ways to destroy one another.

Spiritually dead people cannot change their sin nature. Things change only when they believe that Jesus' death on the cross and His resurrection bring forgiveness of sins. We are made alive spiritually because the Holy Spirit enters human spirits (John 3:5 and Romans 8:9). When this happens, it means that we have *"crossed over from death to life"* (John 5:24). When the Holy Spirit enters our lives, we are born again, and we are truly alive for the first time.

The Holy Spirit enables us live like God desires us to live. Those who have been born again by the Spirit of God have the potential to live as God intended. Jesus not only told Nicodemus that those who are born again by the Spirit will see the Kingdom, but He said that they would enter the Kingdom. Before Moses died, God led him up a mountain where he would be able to see the land that God had promised Israel. Moses, however, only saw the promise. Joshua led the Israelites into the Promised Land. They entered the land and they received the benefits of God's abundant provision for them. Moses only saw the land. He did not benefit from the blessings of the land. When we receive the Holy Spirit, we can enter the promise of God. We can become increasingly like the Lord Jesus Christ and participate in all that He has provided for us.

Seeing the Kingdom changes the way we think, but God doesn't just want us to think differently. He wants us to *live* differently. On Jesus' last night with His disciples, He talked much about the Holy Spirit. He told them, *"But when he, the Spirit of truth, comes, he will guide you into all truth"* (John 16:13). When Jesus said that the Holy Spirit would guide them into truth, He was telling His disciples that the Holy Spirit would not only enable them to know truth but to live it. He does this as we develop a relationship with Him.

Earlier the same night, Jesus said that He would send another Counselor, the Holy Spirit, to those who obey Him (John 14:26). Jesus had developed a close relationship with His disciples. He was now seeking to comfort them because He was leaving. If another came like Jesus, He would also have a close relationship with them the way Jesus did. As we establish and walk in that close relationship with the Holy Spirit, He will lead us to experience life at its fullest. He guides us by giving us an understanding of the Scriptures that will stimulate us to obey them, with His help. In fact, as we gain an understanding of the Scriptures and trust the Holy Spirit to make us fully alive, we have a power source that allows us to live beyond our natural abilities! We are carried by the Holy Spirit into the life that God had intended for us all along. Jesus described it to the woman at the well by saying, *"whoever drinks the water I give them will never thirst.⁵ Indeed, the water I give them will become in them a spring of water welling up to eternal life"* (John 4:14).

Later, when addressing a crowd at the Feast of Tabernacles, Jesus said, *"Whoever believes in me, as Scripture has said, rivers of living water will flow from within them"* (John 7:38). John tells us that when Jesus spoke of rivers or streams of living water, He was talking about the Holy Spirit. What a difference the indwelling Holy Spirit makes. Before we came to know Christ, we couldn't do the right thing, but now we have the life of God dwelling in us by the Holy Spirit, acting like a spiritual artesian well, giving us all we need to live with the character and purpose of Jesus!

The Holy Spirit empowers for service. After the resurrection and prior to His ascension to heaven, Jesus told His disciples that He was sending them, just like His Father had sent Him. Immediately after saying this, Jesus breathed on them and said, *"Receive the Holy Spirit"* (John 20:22). He wanted to let them know that they would enter into their new ministry with God's power resting upon them. Jesus knew that the disciples would fail if they sought to minister by their own strength. How would they do the works Jesus promised if they only used their natural ability? How could they persevere when resistance came? Luke wrote the Gospel of Luke and the Acts of the Apostles. In both, Luke tells us that Jesus told His disciples to wait for the power of the Holy Spirit before they began their ministry (Luke 24:49 and Acts 1:8). As sent ones, they would need the ability of the Holy Spirit to accomplish their tasks, and so do we.

This ability includes a love for the lost (Galatians 5:14) and a boldness to tell others of the saving work of Jesus Christ (Acts 4). The Holy Spirit gives us all we need to fulfill our unique purpose. The Holy Spirit also guides us into truth, by directing us to do the most effective activities.

A number of years ago, Kerry and I were ministering in Africa. I was scheduled to preach. I had prepared a sermon on the impact of unity in the Body of Christ that I really wanted to preach. However, as I prayed, the Holy Spirit indicated that He did not want me to preach that sermon. I argued with Him for a while, but I had no peace. So, I asked what He wanted me to preach. He told me to preach "A New Name for Jacob." I obeyed and preached that sermon.

At the end of the sermon, I asked those who wanted to receive Christ to talk to the pastor after the service and he would pray with them to receive Jesus. Kerry and I were then escorted to the back of the church where we followed the wonderful African custom of shaking everyone's hand. After I shook the last young man's hand, the interpreter told me his story. When he was born, his parents gave him a girl's name. When he went to school, students made fun of him because he had a girl's name. He quit school in fourth grade because of his shame. He finally changed his name legally, but his shame did not go away. He had been going from church to church seeking an answer for his problems, but found none until he heard this message, "A New Name for Jacob." He said he knew the message was for him when I announced the title, which I rarely do. After the service, he went to the pastor and received Jesus, and his shame left immediately. Only the Holy Spirit could know that he would be there, and that he would need that particular message. The Holy Spirit will continually lead us—if we are listening.

The Holy Spirit also gives us discernment that enables us to avoid activities that could waste our time or hurt us in some way. For example, a woman came to a church, where I served on the staff, to receive deliverance. A team of people ministered to the woman, while another team prayed. After the first session, the prayer team shared that they believed God had told them that this woman did not sincerely want help and the team should not meet with her any longer because she had been sent there to distract and to take up time that could be used elsewhere. Motivated by compassion, the deliverance team met with the woman several more times. Even though the woman came for help several more times, she did not gain freedom. Eventually it became clear to everyone that the prayer team had heard the voice of God.

What grace! The Holy Spirit makes us alive, He enables us to live the life God intends for us and He empowers us to fulfill our individual part in advancing God's Kingdom throughout the earth.

4. Jesus Gives Us Like-Minded Believers so We Don't Live Life Alone.

In the 1990s, I pastored a church that was very difficult for me because some of the leaders and congregation had very different ideas about the direction of the church than I did. As a result, I led a number of tense board meetings. I would come home from those meetings emotionally drained. I did not always feel supported, by at least part of the congregation. However, when I came home, I knew that I had unconditional love and support from my wife. This support gave me the courage to keep going.

As we begin to live like sent ones, we must remember that we are not alone. There are others who desire to see Christ's Kingdom advance throughout the earth. These believers understand the opportunities and challenges that we face. For this reason, Jesus' primary command to His disciples was to love one another. He tells them that this is His command (John 13:34-35 and John 15:12,17).

In Summary

God was and is confident that things will be different this time. He sent Jesus not only with the truth, but also with the grace to enable us to obey it. He has taken away our shame. He has made us alive by the Holy Spirit who also empowers us to live this life fully, and helps us fulfill His calling in our lives. I want to mention at this time that there will be a complete chapter on each of the means of grace we have discussed here. Although each of the topics will be expanded, we will repeat some of the material to give a full teaching on the subject. As we talk about these means of grace, we will also talk about how we can access the grace so we can live life at its fullest. These are not just claims. To see how the church is doing see Appendix A.

ENDNOTES

1. http://www.setminds-mindsets.com/mindsets/swiss-watches-set-minds-paradigms-and-mindsets.html; accessed 12/11/2013

2. In one of Jesus' discussions with His opponents, He told them that it is not what goes into the mouth, but what comes out of the mouth (because it reveals what is inside us) that defiles. The comment by Mark means that Jesus lifted the restriction on eating certain foods (Mark 7:19).

3. The scope of this book does not allow us to develop this theme thoroughly. However, the Scriptures teach us that God is One (Deuteronomy 6). They also tell us that both Jesus (John 8:58, 10:30) and the Holy Spirit (Acts 5:3-5) are God. This has caused Bible teachers to conclude that God is Three, but One. This doctrine has been called the Trinity. The author holds to this position. We may find this difficult to understand. I do as well. However, if we could understand God completely, He would have to be less than or equal to us. We don't need a God that small.

4. The tithe is 10 percent. The Scriptures indicate that God wants our giving to begin with 10 percent. See Malachi 3:7-10.

5. He will be satisfied and never need anything else to meet those deep needs.

CHAPTER SIX

Law Versus Grace

We have seen in previous chapters that God has planned an abundant life for us. He has not only revealed the kind of life He desires for us to live, but He has provided the means by which we may live that life. As exciting as this is, not every believer takes advantage of God's provision. As a result, some believers fall short of the life God intended for them.

The remainder of the book discusses how we can live a life that increasingly becomes more like the life God has planned for us. Before we can talk about that, though, we must explore a subject that has been debated for centuries. The question is, "What role does obedience play in accessing God's grace?"

In the sixteenth century, Martin Luther received a revelation from God that we are justified by faith alone, a truth that had been hidden from most believers. At the time of Luther's new understanding of Scripture, he had been part of the Catholic church, the only church of his day. Catholics believe in purgatory, a place defined as a "purification, so as to achieve the holiness necessary to enter the joy of heaven," which is experienced by those "who die in God's grace and friendship, but still imperfectly purified" (CCC 1030).[1] At the time, the Catholic church allowed monetary gifts, called indulgences, which could shorten the time spent in purgatory.[2]

As a result of his new revelation, and the prevailing practice of indulgences, Luther vehemently opposed anything that appeared to suggest that works could assist in accomplishing our salvation. Luther felt so strongly about salvation being completely by faith, that he did not accept the Book of James as inspired Scripture because James insisted that the only real demonstration of faith is works.[3] Luther's insistence that salvation is only by faith, changed the course of the world. Because he wanted to bring correction to what he perceived to be false doctrine, Luther took a strong stand concerning the doctrine of faith with church leaders. The church of Luther's time rejected his premise, which forced him to leave the Catholic church. He later established the Lutheran church, which led to the development of the entire Protestant Movement.[4] Had James and Luther, two great men of God, been in the same room, they would have disagreed passionately with each other.

We continue to debate this subject in a variety of ways in our day. I will discuss a few of the common arguments on the subject and lay out for you what I believe is the proper biblical understanding of the subject. This forms the foundation for the remainder of the book.

"We are saved by works." This position may take many forms, but essentially declares that people must fulfill the will of God on their own if they are to experience salvation. This position is summed up by saying, "If my good deeds exceed my bad deeds, I will go to heaven," or "If I accomplish certain works or perform the right rituals during my lifetime, I will go to heaven." We have already seen that men and women left to their own devices do not fulfill the will of God. Moses told us that even the inclinations of our heart are continuously evil (Genesis 6:5) and Jeremiah indicated that humans are so wicked that their own hearts deceive them (Jeremiah 17:9). The writer of Ecclesiastes reminds us that *"There is no one on earth who is righteous, no one does what is right and never sins"* (Ecclesiastes 7:20). Paul could not be clearer when he declares, *"he saved us, not because of righteous things we had done, but because of his mercy"* (Titus 3:5).

In other words, we cannot be saved by our own works, but only by the mercy of God. Jesus said that He gives life to those who believe that His death on the cross paid the penalty for our sin, that He rose from the grave to provide newness of life, and that He ascended to heaven to be with the Father to take His final place of authority—to enable those He sent to fulfill their ministries (John 5:19-24).

The fact that we cannot be saved by our own efforts is confirmed at Gethsemane. When faced with the horrifying prospect of dying on a Roman cross, Jesus asked His Father if there was another way. God had no other way to bring forgiveness of sin. The Lamb of God had to pay sin's penalty. The writer of Hebrews tells us that the Old Testament sacrifices did not bring newness of life to the people of Israel. The sacrifices had to be made every year, which reminded them that they were sinful and it left them in their shame (Hebrews 10:1-9). However, he tells us that Jesus' sacrifice was sufficient for all time. He died once for all (Hebrews 10:10). Not only have believers been forgiven of all their sin, but they have also been given a new life through the indwelling Holy Spirit (John 3:3,5 and Romans 8:1-4 remind us of this fact). If there had been another way, surely the Father would have spared His only Son.

It is unlikely that James would disagree with Luther's conclusion that we are saved by grace through faith. James, the brother of Jesus,[5] did not believe in Jesus when He ministered on the earth, but later he became a believer and the leader of the church at Jerusalem (Acts 15:13). He stayed true to his belief in Jesus even though he was stoned to death for his faith.[6] He had become a changed man. The only explanation is that he had been born again. However, if James believed that we are saved by grace through faith, what could he have meant when he said that works demonstrate faith (James 2:18)?

I want to make a few things clear at this point. Merely saying the words to the "sinner's prayer" does not guarantee that a person has been born again. In the first church Kerry and I pastored, we continually heard wives tell us that their husbands "loved the Lord." Although our goal was to produce people who love the Lord, we came to realize that what these women meant was that their husbands, at one point had gone to the altar and repeated the words to the sinner's prayer, but their lives gave no demonstration that anything had changed. They rarely attended church or participated in any Kingdom work.

I am not saying that we are saved by some combination of faith and certain works, nor am I saying that church attendance or other "Christian" activities save us. I am saying that if we have been saved by faith, there should be some change in our lives that demonstrates that we are not the same person anymore. This is exactly what James meant. His statement that we will show our faith by our works tells us that he believed that if we have truly been born again, there will be a change in our lives. The saved person may be convicted by areas of sin that did not bother him or her before, or the person may experience a hunger to become more like Jesus that leads to a major lifestyle change. Or, the newly born-again person may dedicate him or herself to the purposes of God, instead of living only for self. In other words, a believer's works should visibly demonstrate that the person has exercised faith in the finished work of Christ and is no longer the same person. Praise God, He changes us!

Before I was married, I did not keep my home very neat; but after I married Kerry, whom I loved (and I still do) and wanted to please in every way, I knew that if I continued to be messy, she would not be pleased. So I immediately began to use the hamper for my dirty clothes. I changed my mind about who decided what our house would look like. Because my mind changed, my actions changed as well. Our house was neater than mine had been. My change was not because of nagging (she does not nag) but because of love. When we are born again, our lives are under new management. We used to do what we wanted, but now because we love Him, we do what He wants. Our priorities continually change. As our priorities change, so do our actions. Our actions demonstrate that we have been saved.

"We are saved by faith, but after salvation we must obey on our own." We have already discussed Paul's own struggles as he sought to live righteously. He told us that he did what he did not want to, and did not do what he knew was right (Romans 7:14-25). In utter frustration, he cried out, *"Who will rescue me from this body that is subject to death?"* (Romans 7:24). He recognized that when he sought to live for Christ by his own will and intelligence, he acted like he was still dead in his sins. He finally concluded that it is only as we live by the power of the indwelling Holy Spirit, that we can overcome our failure to obey God. If we live by the Spirit's power, we can overcome our sin nature and live the life that God intended for us to live (Romans 8:1-4). This is why Jesus told His disciples to *"stay in the city until you have been clothed with power from on high"* (Luke 24:49). He knew they could never live the Christian life by their own strength. Paul told the believers at Colossae, *"So, then, just as you received Christ Jesus as Lord, continue to live your lives in him"* (Colossians 2:6). They had received Christ by faith. Paul says that now they must continue to live by faith in the One who not only provided for their entrance into the Kingdom, but also makes it possible for them to change the way they live.

"You must keep the rules to be acceptable to God." Some believers reject the concept of obedience to the Lord because they have come out of churches or "Christian" movements that had many rules. Sometimes we call these groups legalistic. Legalism occurs when a church or organization has a set of rules that each believer must conform to, in order to be acceptable to the organization and, in their

mind, to God. Paul confronted legalism when a group of ethnic Jews, who had become believers in Christ, acknowledged that salvation comes by faith in Jesus Christ, but demanded that all believers keep certain aspects of the Jewish Law, such as circumcision, in order to be considered righteous. This became such a major issue in the early Church that a convocation was called to discuss whether these Jewish believers were correct. The conclusion that the convocation came to is interesting. Basically, they determined that the Gentile believers did not need to keep the ceremonial aspects of the Law.[7] They determined that the Gentile believers should abstain from sexual immorality. If we believe the Bible, we agree with this decision. We must be sexually pure in order to walk in righteousness. However, they also asked the Gentile believers not to eat meat with blood in it or meat sacrificed to idols.

The first requirement seems right, but is it really sin to eat rare meat (I must admit that I personally like to know that the animal is dead when I eat it!) or eat meat that has been sacrificed to an idol? Paul actually told the believers in Corinth that he did not believe it is wrong to eat meat sacrificed to idols (1 Corinthians 8:4-6), but he goes on to say that he will never eat meat sacrificed to an idol, if it will offend someone. A person is offended when he or she is so distraught by the actions of another believer, that their faith is shaken, even to the point of walking away from the Lord. Paul stated that he would not knowingly participate in an activity that would have a negative impact upon the faith of another. The leaders at Jerusalem added eating meat with blood in it, because the Law had been preached in so many places. These leaders said, "Eat your meat well done so that you do not hinder Jews, or Gentiles who have converted to Judaism, from listening to your preaching and coming to faith in Jesus." You may prefer your meat rare, but is it worth hindering someone from coming to Christ? The same is true of meat offered to idols.

The general rule is that we do not want to put restrictions upon believers that are not recorded in Scripture. However, we must realize that at times, even though we have the freedom in Christ to engage in certain activities, we should voluntarily abstain from them so that we don't cause an offence to a weaker brother or someone who has not yet come to Christ. For, example, you may develop a relationship with Muslim neighbors. In order to show your love, and perhaps gain an opportunity to share Jesus, you invite them for a meal. When you have them over, you will assure them that you will not serve wine, pork, or shell fish. You may personally participate in all or some of these, but Muslims are forbidden to eat or drink them. You refrain from exercising your freedom because of your love for others.

You may wonder why I have included this material. It is because those who are legalistic believe that their rules and regulations are part of righteous behavior. Many of these legalistic laws may have started out because of love. Some may have determined that they should not engage in an activity because they wanted to reach someone or some group of people. At some point, however, the activity no longer caused an offense, but the group continued to abstain and required others to do so.

Before I became a pastor, I served on the board of my church. My pastor decided that he would build a relationship with one of the teenage men in the congregation. They went out to spend some time together and went to a pool hall. The young man's grandmother was upset that the pastor would take her grandson to a pool hall. Evidently that was taboo in her mind. However, in this case, the pool hall didn't sell alcohol, and there were no barroom girls to bring distraction or temptation. Staying away from a pool hall may have been a good idea at one time, but this was no longer true in this case. Let's do things out of love, but let's not make the behavior a test of righteousness for all time, unless the Scriptures say so, as in the case of sexual immorality discussed previously. Legalism adds to the Gospel, but love requires that we give up what we have the freedom to do for the benefit of others.

We must also determine how we will live with believers who differ on issues that are not part of the core values of the faith. Some believers may feel that you should wear a suit and tie to church, while others are perfectly comfortable worshiping in jeans and a tee shirt. Some believers have a glass of wine with a meal, while others believe it is sin to do so. It seems to me that as we mature in our walk with the Lord, we will know how to walk in unity in these situations. If we are fellowshipping with mature believers, we will learn to be comfortable with brothers and sisters who engage in activities that we do not. The shoe will be on the other foot as well. We may do things that other mature believers do not, but they fellowship with us because the Christian life is about loving Jesus and loving others, not getting other believers to live like we do in every detail. We serve the same Lord, and we are actively seeking to advance His Kingdom. For the mature believer, these non-core issues do not divide us.

If we are with young or immature believers who do not believe that Christians should engage in certain activities, we should abstain so that we do not shatter their faith. As we fellowship with them, many of them will become mature as we sacrificially love them. In addition, if we are fellowshipping with a recovering alcoholic, we will be careful to abstain from all alcoholic beverages in order to help them overcome their addictions and grow in the Lord. In that same way, we will want to consider which movies we suggest, if we are with someone who has come out of a pornography addiction.

As a speaker, I usually ask the church, who has invited me, to tell me what is appropriate to wear in their church. I speak in churches where a suit is appropriate. I speak in others where it may actually detract from the message. Seek to determine Jesus' unchanging truths and keep them by the power of the Holy Spirit. When it comes to other areas, participate if you have the freedom unless it will damage the faith of another.

I have this word for those who struggle with legalism: Please do not put requirements upon people that God does not require. There may be some things we suggest that others do or do not do because we perceive that they will keep them from fulfilling God's will. However, remember that these are only suggestions, not a test of spirituality. We will not come to complete agreement on every issue, so we must learn to fellowship with those who differ in noncore issues. Each of us is only one part of one Body charged with taking the Gospel to the ends of the earth.

"Grace-Grace." This is a term that my wife and I use to describe a particular attitude that seems to be prevalent among many Christians in our day. Let me explain by using an illustration. A number of years ago, Kerry invited a woman to our home for lunch because the woman was interested in one of our international trips. As they talked, the woman shared that she had had many boyfriends and had been married previously. She had divorced her first husband and married again about a year prior to meeting Kerry. She said the second marriage was not going well either. Then she said, "Oh well, if it doesn't work out, God will forgive me." I do not share this story to denigrate the forgiving power of God. As we view Old Testament history of the nation of Israel, we see God forgiving over and over, even when the nation had forsaken God and worshiped other gods. At one point, we see God illustrating His indomitable love through the prophet Hosea. God told Hosea to marry a prostitute who eventually left him to go into prostitution. God told Hosea to find her and pay the price to buy her back. God then declared, "This is what my unrelenting love is like. This is how I forgive. This is how I seek you to do all I can to give you the wonderful life that I had planned for you from the beginning." (See the Book of Hosea.)

I shared the story of the woman, not to question God's desire to forgive no matter what we do, but because the woman seemed flippant about the failure of her marriage. Of course, He will forgive, but I believe that there should be a certain level of grief that the marriage had failed or repentance for any sin on her part that may have contributed to the marital problems. God does not want any marriage to fail. It seems to me that the proper attitude should have been, "Lord, change anything in me that contributes to the failure of my marriage. Lord, would You please do what is necessary to make the marriage work, in order to bring glory to You." I admit that there are times when a marriage does not work out. I certainly do not condemn those who have gone through divorce. I told the story to show the sad misunderstanding of the grace of God and the need to seek the Lord to do what He can to save the marriage or bring victory in an area.

Those with the grace-grace attitude recognize that God forgives our sins. This is important, because if we don't know about His grace, we can never get past the shame of our sin to reach the abundant life that God has planned for us. Earlier in my marriage, when our children were young, I would sometimes become angry at them, often for very minor things. After I had expressed my anger, I would feel guilty and discouraged, feeling that I was not worthy to be a servant of God or to serve as a pastor. It was difficult to boldly seek to advance the Kingdom of God when I was in this state. After some time, the Holy Spirit highlighted a Scripture to me:

> *Brothers and sisters, I do not consider myself yet to have taken hold of it. But one thing I do: Forgetting what is behind and straining toward what is ahead, I press on toward the goal to win the prize for which God has called me heavenward in Christ Jesus* (Philippians 3:13-14).

I learned two principles from this passage. First, Paul believed that when God forgave him, it was complete. He did not need to wallow in guilt and shame. It doesn't matter what we have done in the past, God can forgive us and change us. Paul illustrates this for us. Before giving his life to Christ, he persecuted followers of Jesus and had them imprisoned. He repented and God forgave him.

The second principle we see in this passage is that we should not let the sins of our past keep us from moving into the future God has planned for us. God forgives. He doesn't even remember them. David told us, *"as far as the east is from the west, so far has he removed our transgressions from us"* (Psalm 103:12). As far as God is concerned, our sins are removed when we repent. *He does not remember them.* Therefore, Paul says, "I will not let the sin and shame of my past rob me of the future that God has from me. So, I repent, seek God to help me overcome the sin, and move forward to accomplish all that God has for me." Paul demonstrates that this advice works, because he became the greatest missionary of all time, as well as the writer of much of the New Testament. When God highlighted this passage to me, I began to find it easier to live and minister in victory, knowing that He had forgiven me and that He was seeking to make me more like Jesus.

As I mentioned in Chapter 4, my wife and I met Kamal Saleem.[8] Kamal had been a terrorist, smuggling arms into Israel for the Palestine Liberation Organization (PLO) to use against Jews when he was seven years old. Kamal continued to engage in various types of jihad until he had a horrible traffic accident, which brought him into contact with some believers who exemplified Jesus. After a long struggle, Kamal surrendered his life to Jesus and today boldly preaches the Gospel.[9] Kamal did not let his past keep him from his God-ordained calling. Neither should we. We should repent of our sins, seek God's forgiveness and victory and forge ahead to do what He has called us to do.

The problem with some who take the grace-grace position is that they don't think it is a big deal when they sin. They don't understand that their sin is a hindrance to glorifying the Lord (more on this in a later chapter). Paul ran into people with a similar attitude. They recognized that when they sinned, God demonstrated His grace by forgiving them. They asked, *"What shall we say then? Shall we go on sinning so that grace may increase?"* Paul responded, *"By no means!*

We are those who have died to sin; how can we live in it any longer?" (Romans 6:1-2). When Paul says, *"By no means,"* he used language that may be too strong in English to print in this book. Stronger than "Heck no!" To put it mildly, Paul did not think we should go on sinning. He said, *"We have died to sin."* This is why Paul could press forward. God not only supplies the grace to give us forgiveness for our sins, but He gives us the ability to gain victory over these sins so we can live a new life, looking more like Jesus.

When we met Kamal Saleem, we expected to see someone hardened by his past. However, when we looked into his eyes, we saw Jesus. He is no longer the hate-filled terrorist, but a person who exudes the love of Jesus.

God wants to forgive each of us. He wants us to realize that our past, present, and future sins have been forgiven, so that we no longer live with the stain of guilt and shame. The reason He wants us to be free from guilt and shame is so we can live the life He has planned for us, which includes becoming increasingly like Jesus Christ and fulfilling our God-ordained destiny in advancing God's Kingdom throughout the earth.

Those who maintain the grace-grace position often focus upon themselves. They rightly believe that God will forgive their sin, which means no sin stands between them and God. They are confident that they will someday spend eternity with God, but some don't seem to recognize that failing to allow God to change their lives might reflect badly upon Jesus and His work. They don't seem to recognize that if their lives don't change after they receive Jesus, nonbelievers may reject Him. They also don't seem to realize that when they fail to change, they don't become all that Jesus desires them to be, and they fail to minister as broadly as He desires.

Salvation is not just about being forgiven and spending eternity with God. It is about becoming fully alive! We are fully alive when our lives are becoming more like His and we are walking in His purposes for us.

OBEDIENCE

Becoming more fully alive brings us to the issue of obedience. John uses the words "obey, obeyed, and obeys" nine times in his Gospel. He uses the word "command" another six times in referring to commands that Jesus gave to His disciples, and the word "commanded" four times when He talks about how He obeyed His Father. On several occasions, Jesus ties promises to our obedience: The Holy Spirit will be given to the obedient (John 14:15-16); the Father and Son will reveal themselves to the obedient (John 14:21,23); and joy will be given to the obedient (John 15:11). In John 8, Jesus says that those who follow Him (implying obedience) will know truth at a level that will set them free. In John 15, Jesus tells us that those who remain in Him, and who allow His Word to live in them (A level of obedience and discipline is implied here. We will talk about this in great detail in the coming chapters.) will be able to pray for anything in His name, and see answers (John 15:1-8).

We have already established that we cannot obey God on our own, but these Scriptures indicate that much of our blessing is dependent upon our obedience. Moses tells the Israelites the same thing when he lays out the activities that bring blessing and the ones that bring curses (Deuteronomy 26–28). However, as we have seen, Israel continually failed. Does this imply that there is some sinister plot by God to dangle blessings in front of us knowing that we will never receive them? Are we doomed to know what life could be, but miserably fail to live that life? Is it even possible to be fully alive?

John gives us the answer in his first letter:

Dear friends, I am not writing you a new command but an old one, which you have had since the beginning. This old command

is the message you have heard. Yet I am writing you a new com-
mand; its truth is seen in him and in you, because the darkness
is passing and the true light is already shining (1 John 2:7-8).

This seems like some kind of double talk. The same command is old, but it is new. There is a solution to the dilemma. When the command to love one another (1 John 2:9) was originally given in the Law, the people had to fulfill the command by their own power. They could not! However, the command is new because God has now provided the means of grace discussed in Chapter 5, to enable believers to do what they cannot do on their own.

In Summary

We cannot live the life God desires in our own ability. The Law is good, but powerless because of humankind's inability to do what is right. However, when we are born again, the Holy Spirit comes into our lives, and gives us God's perspective on life, and the power to live that life. This new nature longs to know Jesus and be like Him. As we allow the Holy Spirit to work in our lives, He enables us to obey. When we obey, we get more of the Holy Spirit (John 14:15-16), develop an intimate walk with the Father and Son (John 14:21,23), and live in joy (John 15:11). I wanted to discuss this subject before we went on because the remainder of the book is a call to be disciplined. It is a call to obedience. I wanted you to see that although we are called to obey, God has given us every spiritual resource to enable us to do that.

ENDNOTES

1. http://www.catholic.com/tracts/purgatory; accessed 1/8/2014.

2. http://www.haciendapub.com/randomnotes/martin-lu-ther-sale-indulgences-and-reformation; accessed 1/7/2014.

3. http://www.biblestudy.org/question/why-did-martin-luther-want-book-of-james-out-of-bible.html; accessed 1/7/2014.

4. The Protestant Movement eventually established the modern Missions Movement. The result is that many more believers took up their role as sent ones.

5. David P. Nystrom, The NIV Application Commentary: James (Grand Rapids, MI: Zondervan Publishing House, 1997), 19-21.

6. Ajith Fernando, The NIV Application Commentary: James (Grand Rapids, MI: Zondervan Publishing House, 1998), 417.

7. We acknowledge that this only included the ceremonial aspects. As we have concluded previously, the moral requirements of the Law are basically the same as New Testament truth.

8. Not his real name for purposes of safety.

9. Read Kamal's story in *Kamal Saleem—The Blood of Lambs* (New York: Howard Books, a division of Simon and Schuster, 2009).

SECTION II

CALLED TO OBEY

Intimacy with God

Before, we begin chapter seven, I want to summarize some of the points that we've already covered in Section 1.

We've described God's great love for all people that motivated Him to create an abundant plan for them. We've read of His plan for humanity and His unrelenting love that never gave up on them even when they rejected Him. We also saw that God set in motion a plan that would enable humans to fulfill His plan for their lives.

Our brief look at the current state of the Church, in Appendix A, told us that many believers have lived the kind of purpose-filled life that God intended. We saw that the Church grew from a small number of followers of Jesus to more than one billion in our day. These one billion believers are scattered worldwide, and many of them are seeking to bring the life Jesus offers to others. There have been missionaries, like the apostle Paul, who took the Gospel where no one else had preached,[2] and R.A. Jaffrey who effectively ministered in

China and later opened up ministry on two islands in what is now Indonesia.[3] Others, like Bob Pierce, who founded World Vision, and Franklin Graham, who founded Samaritan's Purse, touch millions through their benevolent ministries and support of the local church around the world. Of course, there have been thousands of others, most of whom we have never heard, who have gone across the sea and across the street, advancing the Kingdom of God. Women like Amy Carmichael who spent 56 years in India and men like Reverend Harold Sipe and Reverend Reynold Waltimyer who spent time with a young believer named John Shuey. Through their mentoring, these two men touched people on four continents, even though Reverend Sipe now lives in heaven and Reverend Waltimyer has retired from pastoral ministry.

Many unsung heroes like Reverends Sipe and Waltimyer have ministered in cities and villages through the ages, marching to the beat of the Holy Spirit's leading, advancing the Kingdom of God. Some of these brave "sent ones" remain faithful and effective even under the most severe circumstances; men like Pastor Saeed Abedini, an Iranian-born U.S. citizen, who was thrown into Evin prison in Tehran for his faith. While in this prison, he led at least 30 inmates to Christ.[4] Pastor Abedini remains in prison and has been transferred to an even worse prison.[5] He suffers for Christ because he will not deny Him.

Jesus died to save men and women so they can walk in intimacy with God and live life at its fullest. People who live to advance His Kingdom on earth are called disciples of the Lord Jesus Christ. God's desire is to have an ever-expanding core of disciples touching the lives of others with the Good News until the world is changed.

I must admit, with some perplexity, that I have seen many who claim to be disciples of Jesus, yet they partially or completely fail to live as God desires.

The second section of this book outlines ways we can access God's grace so we can live a life that is truly fully alive. Remember in Chapter One we described being fully alive this way:

We are fully alive when we live the best life we can live. It is a life where we have been forgiven of all our sins by God, been born again into a new life, and have entered into a life-long intimate relationship with Him. The new life begins when our sins are forgiven, and we become connected to God through the finished work of Jesus Christ. We literally have the life of Jesus living in us! Therefore, we live a joy-filled, righteous life where we play a role in advancing God's Kingdom throughout the earth. When we live life like this, we are *Fully Alive.*

WALKING IN INTIMACY WITH GOD

I am including a large passage of Scripture because it is foundational to what we will discuss in this chapter and the remainder of the book. Please read the following passage.

I am the true vine, and my Father is the gardener. He cuts off every branch in me that bears no fruit, while every branch that does bear fruit he prunes so that it will be even more fruitful. You are already clean because of the word I have spoken to you. Remain in me, as I also remain in you. No branch can bear fruit by itself; it must remain in the vine. Neither can you bear fruit unless you remain in me. I am the vine; you are the branches. If you remain in me and I in you, you will bear much fruit; apart from me you can do nothing. If you do not remain in me, you are like a branch that is thrown away and withers; such branches are picked up, thrown into the fire and burned. If you remain in me and my words remain in you, ask whatever you wish, and it will be done for you. This is to my Father's glory, that you bear much fruit, showing yourselves to be my disciples. As the Father has loved me, so have I loved you.

Now remain in my love. If you keep my commands, you will remain in my love, just as I have kept my Father's commands and remain in his love. I have told you this so that my joy may be in you and that your joy may be complete. My command is this: Love each other as I have loved you. Greater love has no one than this: to lay down one's life for one's friends. You are my friends if you do what I command. I no longer call you servants, because a servant does not know his master's business. Instead, I have called you friends, for everything that I learned from my Father I have made known to you. You did not choose me, but I chose you and appointed you so that you might go and bear fruit—fruit that will last—and so that whatever you ask in my name the Father will give you (John 15:1-16).

THE VINE AND THE BRANCHES

When we first moved to our current home, there was a large apple orchard beside our development. Each fall we saw thousands of apples hanging on the trees. However, the apples only grew and thrived on branches that remained attached to the tree. Branches that broke off did not produce apples. This reminds us that life comes from the roots into the trunk of the tree and then into the branches. Branches only have life as long as they are connected to the tree.

In this passage, Jesus says He is the Vine. He is the source of life. John tells us that Jesus had life in Himself (John 1:4). He has life because He is God. He has always had life and always will. The psalmist declared, *"from everlasting to everlasting you are God"* (Psalm 90:2). It has already been discussed that when we are born again, the Holy Spirit enters our human spirit, opening the connection between us and God that was severed when Adam and Eve sinned. Humans, were created by God, who is the Gardener, to be part of the Vine, but were separated from God through disobedience. However, those who have received Jesus Christ into their lives have been reconnected to God, the vine. (See Romans 11:17 for further instruction on this subject.)

As branches, we can only bear fruit when we stay connected to the Vine. When we were born again, the conduit between us and God was opened. As we remain in Jesus, His life courses through us in a way that enables us to bear fruit. When we are connected to Jesus, we bear two types of fruit. First, we become like Jesus in character. The fruit of the Holy Spirit, described by Paul in Galatians 5:22-23, is the character of Jesus manifested in and through our lives. Second, as we become more like Jesus, we will minister in a way that has an impact upon others. When we are like Jesus, we will seek to help others live the abundant life God desires for them. Because we are more like Him, we will act more like Him. Regardless of our past, God's desire is to make us like Jesus, and to use us to touch others. We are meant to be fruit-bearers!

YOU ARE ALREADY CLEAN

Richard Lenski's Commentary on the New Testament says that when Jesus told the disciples that they were already clean, He meant that they had been justified, born again.[6] The severed relationship, thrust upon them by the disobedience of Adam and Eve, was reconnected, and they began a relationship with Jesus Christ. They were connected to God. Every person in every age who has received Jesus Christ by faith, has been connected to Him.

WE MUST REMAIN IN HIM

When we come into a relationship with Jesus, whether we call it being born again, saved, or receiving Jesus, we come into connection with the Father, Son, and Holy Spirit. Before we accepted Jesus as our Savior, we were branches laying on the ground, depending on our own spiritually lifeless abilities to eke out some semblance of life for ourselves. But now we've been connected with God, who is life Himself. We have been given the potential to live life like God intended when He created us.

We are told that we must remain in the Vine in order to reach our potential. In other words, we have been connected to Jesus when our sins, which separated us from God (Isaiah 59:1-2) were forgiven, but we must continue in God's grace through faith, in order to bear fruit and move steadily toward the fullness of our God-given potential. When we do this, we are effectively remaining in Him.

DEVELOPING INTIMACY WITH GOD

God wants us to remain in Him because He desires a relationship with us. This is why John tells us that those who receive Jesus become *"children of God"* (John 1:12). Jesus said that His friends were those who obey Him (John 15:16). God wants us to be in His family and to be Jesus' friend.

As we study the topic of intimacy with God, we realize that He has always intended for humankind to have a relationship with Him. We are not completely restored to Him if we do not possess the kind of relationship that Adam and Eve had with the Father, one in which He walked with them in the *"cool of the day"* (Genesis 3:8). We will never truly live the fullness of life that God desires, unless we walk so closely with Him that we know Him personally, and He gives a revelation of the truth, as written in the Bible, that enables us to live life as He planned. It begins with relationship.

Peter tells us: *"For Christ also suffered once for sins, the righteous for the unrighteous, to bring you to God..."* (1 Peter 3:18). Jesus' sacrificial death on the cross was to obliterate the sin that stood between us and God. When we receive Jesus as Savior and Lord, He brings us to God. As this new relationship begins, a connection develops between us and God, because the Spirit of God enters our human spirit.

In fact, in His prayer at Gethsemane, the night before His crucifixion, Jesus tells us, *"Now this is eternal life: that they know you, the only true God, and Jesus Christ, whom you have sent"* (John 17:3). Eternal life can be defined as knowing the Father and the Son. In fact, John has made it quite clear that unless we know Him, we will never experience real life (John 20:31). When we become believers, a personal relationship is established with God Himself. But like any relationship, we must commit to developing it to see it grow.

My wife and I have been married more than thirty-seven years. We try to communicate with each other multiple times each day. Sometimes it is because we need information, but sometimes I check in to see how her day is going. She does the same with me. The only time we don't communicate daily is when one of us is out of the country without the other, which rarely happens anymore. Even then, we talk as much as possible. In the remaining pages of this chapter, I share some basic suggestions that will help you get started in developing a personal relationship with the Lord, or that will help you develop a stronger relationship with Him.

Set a time and place to meet with God. We are creatures of habit. If we set a particular time and place aside to be with the Lord, it becomes part of our schedule. I have a particular chair in our house where I sit to spend time with Jesus. I have done this as long as I can remember. I admit that I like routine. It is interesting that God sends my wife and me to foreign nations and on weekend retreats where I have little control over the schedule, and our days can rarely be called routine! However, even in these situations when I can't always control my schedule, I seek a place to pray and read, even if it means sitting on the floor in the room where we sleep. Some may say that routine is religious, but don't we do many things routinely? For example, we generally eat our meals at the same time each day. We like to joke that in India, nothings seems to happen on time with the exception of tea time. In addition, if we are presenting a seminar, lunch arrives at the prescribed time. Why? Because we need our nourishment if we are going to have the strength to accomplish the tasks God has given to us. Jesus is our spiritual bread. We need to get to know Him better and better if we are to live life at its fullest.

We may protest that we can't set aside a place and time because our schedules are so busy. Unfortunately, when we are busy, important things can be neglected because we are doing things that are not top priority. This happens, for example, when parents allow the challenges of their work to crowd out time with the children. Before they know it, the children are grown and they realize that they haven't given themselves to the most important thing of spending time with family.

Therefore, wise people schedule their most important activities first, so that less important ones don't crowd them out. I can't imagine a wife being offended if her busy husband said to her, "My schedule has gotten so full, but you are the most important person in my life. I want to schedule times when we can get together throughout the week, and I won't let anything keep me from those times (with the exception of legitimate emergencies)." God won't be offended by this either. Jesus said that we are His friends if we obey Him. Friends hang out. Friends find out what is going on in each others' lives. Friends find out what is important to the other. This is how friends get to know one another.

Having this scheduled time doesn't preclude being spontaneous. Sometimes friends decide on the spur of the moment to do something special or different. You can do this in your relationship with the Lord. You may occasionally move to a different place for your devotional time, or you may add time with Him. You may want to extend your time with the Lord or go to a different place, for instance, when you have a major decision to make. I remember when my wife and I needed to make a decision concerning whether I should attend seminary. Our girls were five and two at the time, and it meant we would be putting ourselves in a position to depend on the Lord. It was a big decision. We were visiting Kerry's parents, and we decided to leave the girls with Nanny and Pappa and go to a nearby park. When we got there, we went our separate ways and sought the Lord. There was something about being in a different place that facilitated making our decision. When we came back together we shared that we both felt the Lord saying "Yes!" We saw God provide for us in many amazing ways during our time in seminary. However, that is the subject of another book!

You may ask, "How much time should I set aside with the Lord?" This answer will vary from person to person. It may also vary, to some degree, depending on your current situation. A mother with young children may need to get creative to get even a little time with the Lord. When our oldest daughter, Kristin, was a baby, Kerry had little time to set aside for the Lord. She asked the Lord to wake her in the middle of the night, one-half hour prior to the time Kristin needed her middle-of-the-night feeding. God was faithful to wake Kerry and she was faithful to spend that time with the Lord, because she wanted and needed to be with Him. When Kristin's schedule got a little more routine, Kerry went back to setting a specific time to be with the Lord.

I also want to mention that there may be times when you spend a little less than the normal time because of an emergency, or because of a change in schedule. I encourage you to get back on schedule as soon as you can, so you don't get into a rut that hinders your walk with the Lord.

I suggest starting with a short amount of time, if you are just beginning to spend time alone with the Lord. When I started, I spent about fifteen minutes each day. However, as time went on I increased my time with Him. We also may need to increase our time with the Lord in order to grow in the Lord or when our ministry increases. This seems counterintuitive, but the greater the ministry, the more time we need with the Lord.

The following are some activities you may want to include in your time alone with God. There is no particular order, or even a specific percentage of time you should spend on each. This is your time with the Lord, but I believe each of these activities will enhance your time with Him.

Spend time in praise and thanks. Praise involves honoring God for the greatness of His character. Whenever we see a heavenly scene in the Scriptures, we find angelic beings engaging in praise, as they express their awe of His greatness. (See Isaiah 6:3; Revelation 4:8-11, 5:9-13; and Psalm 145:1-3 for examples of praise.) Some folks actually love to take a hymnbook or worship book with them to assist them to praise. You may want to sing. However, make sure the expressions are yours so you are telling God how amazed you are by Him and how much you honor Him.

Thanksgiving involves thanking God for what He has done in our lives. He has done some amazing things for us, like saving us from sin and giving us a new life. He gives us victory over sin. He also does smaller things for us on a day-to-day basis, like the time our car needed a major repair while I attended seminary. We had to decide whether we would get a new part or a rebuilt one. During the time we were praying about the situation, someone sent us a sizable check. The person didn't know we needed a car repair, and I don't think this person gave to us at any other time during our time at seminary. God continually takes care of situations in our lives. We should want to express our thanks to God for all that He has done for us.

Spend time in God's Word, the Bible. If we truly want to learn truth, we will spend time in the Word of God. Jesus tells us that God's Word is truth (John 17:17). We get to know God as we read the Word. First, we see direct statements that He makes about Himself, such as He is holy, love, and full of mercy. We also get to know Him as we observe how He works in the lives of those whose lives are recorded for us in His Word. For instance, we see the mercy of God as He continually forgives Israel, and seeks to work with her (Hosea is a great example of this). We see His great power to get us out of difficult situations as we observe Him opening the Red Sea (Exodus 14) and as He gives Peter an angelic escape from prison (Acts 12). We also learn how God thinks about particular situations as we read what He says about everything from sex and marriage, to business and religion.

We may wonder how much we should read. When I started, I read ten verses a day and asked God to speak to me. As you read His Word, God will speak to you, which will give you a hunger for more. I suggest that believers begin to work toward reading the Bible once each year. It takes about fifteen to thirty minutes, depending on how fast you read, or how much time you spend meditating upon the passage. Start small. It is better to be consistent with a small amount of Scripture than to read a large portion and then not read for several days or weeks. The Word of God is our spiritual food. We would not think about having a large meal on Sunday and then not eating for the rest of the week.

Here are some questions you may want to ask God as you read:

- Is there some new truth or aspect of Yourself You want to reveal to me?

- What is Your will concerning this decision I must make?

- Is there some sin I need to confess?

Obey what God tells you, as you read His Word. One of the best ways to get to know Jesus is to obey His Word. He tells us that He and the Father reveal themselves to those who obey Him (John 14:21,23). This happens for two reasons: First, if we are obedient, He knows that we are trustworthy and the kind of people He can entrust with more of Himself. Second, He knows that we will understand the Word much better when we experience it. In our ministry reports, we sometimes talk about the slums of Mumbai, India. As we do, we know that most people think of the slums in U.S. inner cities. These can be horrible. However, most middle class people of India live in homes like our American slums. We are not critical of people who do not understand, because it is impossible to understand without experiencing it.

It is this way with God. We know that He is our Supplier. He promises to take care of every need, but that is different from giving a tithe of your pay to the Lord and seeing Him miraculously provide for a bill you could not pay because you gave. We really get to know Him when we experience His work in our lives.

Engage in petition and intercession. This is the asking part of prayer. You have engaged in prayer when you gave praise and thanks, but petition and intercession involve making requests of God. Petition is when you pray for your needs. You know what those needs are. Paul told us that we can ask God about anything (Philippians 4:4-6). Intercession involves praying for others. You will want to be involved in petition and intercession throughout the day, but I suggest that you make it part of your daily time alone with the Lord.

Keep a journal. While on the phone one day, I was given the name of a man I needed to contact. It was not a common name, so I thought I would remember it and did not write it down. I forgot the man's name! We forget more than we think we will, so it's a good idea to write things down—like the truths He teaches you from the Word, the sins He has convicted you to repent of, and important prayer requests. When we write our prayer requests, we can write how He answered. You can go back and review your journal when you need encouragement.

These are some suggestions to help you get started. I believe all the pieces are important, but you must choose the activities that will help you get to know God. We have the privilege of having God mentor and direct us throughout our lives. What a great privilege. So get started!

IN SUMMARY

Jesus wants us to be fully alive. This begins by being connected with God, which happens when we receive Christ into our lives. He tells us that we will have fruitful lives when we stay connected to Him. He tells us that Jesus will be our Friend and give us His joy. We will go into greater detail concerning how to remain in Him and the benefits that come our way as we do.

ENDNOTES

1. We find 120 waiting in the Upper Room for the Father's promise (Acts 1), and we see the resurrected Jesus appearing to 500 at once (1 Corinthians 15:6).

2. 2 Corinthians 10:16.

3. http://www.cmalliance.org/about/history/jaffray; accessed 1/9/2014.

4. http://www.religiontoday.com/blog/pastor-saeed-abedini-leads-30-to-christ-iranian-prison.html; accessed 1/9/2014.

5. To read more of American Pastor Saeed Abedini's plight, visit the American Center for Law and Justice Website: aclj.org.

6. R.C.H. Lenski, *The Interpretation of St. John's Gospel* (Minneapolis, MN: Augsburg Publishing House, 1943), 1031.

CHAPTER EIGHT

Commit Your Life Fully to Jesus

Back when I first entered pastoral ministry, a question would inevitably come up when I met another pastor for the first time. After a short amount of time, the pastor would ask, "How many people attend your church?" As I look back, it seems that the question was meant to be some kind of measuring device to assess my success or to determine where I stood in an unofficial pecking order. At the time, my wife and I led the smallest church in our denomination's district that had members. Consequently, I felt like I was at the bottom of the barrel, where most rookies start.

Although the number of persons attending a church may give some indication of effectiveness, Jesus' ministry indicated that He was not looking for numbers alone. He chose those to whom He could entrust Himself.

After Jesus turned the water into wine (John 2:1-11), His popularity began to increase. Although many people began to follow Jesus, we find that He was not looking for just anyone who believed in Him. He was looking for a specific kind of person, the kind who would truly experience life at its fullest.

> *Now while he was in Jerusalem at the Passover Festival, many people saw the signs he was performing and believed in his name. But **Jesus would not entrust himself to them**, for he knew all people* (John 2:23-24).

Many saw Jesus' miraculous signs and believed in Him. Because of the miracles, Jesus began to attract a gathering, many of whom believed that He was the Prophet-King. However, John tells us that Jesus did not entrust Himself to them, because He knew people's hearts. Interestingly, the word translated "entrust," in the New International Version, is the exact same Greek word translated "believed" in the previous verse. We might say that the passage tells us that "some people believed in Jesus but He did not believe in them,"[1] at least not enough to give them large amounts of His limited time.

We might ask why Jesus would not entrust Himself to a group of people who *"believed in"* Him. I believe that Jesus was and is not just looking for "converts"; He is looking for converts who want to live their lives fully for Him. He is looking for those desiring to be righteous men and women who will be sent by the Father to proclaim the Gospel.

Being born again by the Spirit of God is essential to life in Christ. We cannot see, let alone enter the Kingdom of God, without it (John 3:3,5). However, the purpose of conversion is not *just* so we can be guaranteed a place in heaven, but so we can experience the life God desires while we live on earth. Paul put it succinctly when he wrote, *"For this very reason, Christ died and returned to life so that he might be the Lord of both the dead and the living"* (Romans 14:9).

In other words, Jesus saves sinners so that He might be their Lord. He wants a people who recognize that they have been created to be like Him, and to live for Him. He did not die merely to provide a "fire insurance" policy. Because He is Lord, those who have been born again will do what He asks them to do. In order for them to live this life for Jesus, His followers will access all the means of grace that Jesus has given. Their character will change and they will be used to advance the Kingdom of God. Jesus saves people so they will be restored to God's original plan for them to take His message to the ends of the earth. In fact, believers are not fully alive unless they are growing in grace in such a way that they are becoming like Jesus, and fulfilling the mandate to advance His Kingdom to the ends of the earth. As we will see later, God has a specific plan for each believer, which uniquely suits every believer to play a role in Kingdom advance.

For this reason, Jesus looked for those who would follow Him no matter what He asked them to do, or no matter what came their way as a result of their obedience. We see Jesus' resolve to choose the right kind of people the day He fed the 5,000. They saw the miracles and wanted to be with Him. They listened to Him teach and minister for hours. With typical Asian hospitality, He wanted to feed them because they had gone many hours without eating. The disciples concluded that the cost would be too great, but Jesus fed them after blessing a boy's small lunch. When the crowd saw the miracle, they concluded that Jesus was the Prophet-King, and they wanted to make Him king, so Jesus left (John 6:1-15). These "followers" understood that He was the One who had been promised. They believed that He was the Messiah who would come, ascend to the throne of Israel, break off their yoke of slavery to Rome, and once again make Israel the center of the geo-political world. They did not recognize that Jesus desired to establish a different kind of Kingdom. Jesus told Pilate that *"My kingdom is not of this world"* (John 18:36).

Building *His* Kingdom—Not Our Own

Even in our day, some fail to understand what Jesus desires to accomplish in our world. Some, especially in the U.S., believe that God wants to make them rich. God, however, never promises us the "American Dream," or to make us rich. He *does* promise to meet our needs and He *does* tell us that He gives back even more than we give (Luke 6:36-38), but does He do this so we can live lavishly while other believers live in poverty? Or does He do this so that faithful followers of Jesus will have even more to give to the advancement of the Kingdom of God? Some have concluded and preached that everything should go well for all who have received Christ. Yet we see fully committed people being tortured in prison cells or having their homes burned down by those who oppose them. Perhaps those who hold to these positions are building their own kingdom instead of the Kingdom of God—the place where He rules and reigns!

Jesus does have a Kingdom. He wants that Kingdom to spread worldwide. He knows that when that happens, people from every nation and ethnic group will bow to Him, allowing Him to make their cities and villages the righteous, God-worshiping places He intends for them to be. However, it is a Kingdom built upon the truth proclaimed by Jesus, not one that comes from human reasoning.

There was a second group of "followers" of Jesus who got it wrong the day Jesus fed the 5,000. After ministering all day, Jesus told the disciples to get into a boat and go to the other side of the lake. He did not go with them because He wanted to stay behind so He could spend time with His Father. Later, Jesus joined His disciples by walking on the water until He reached their boat. The crowds, however, did not know that Jesus was with the disciples. They got into boats and rowed to the place Jesus had last been seen. Of course, they did not find Him there, so they rowed to where Jesus and His disciples had gone. These "followers" worked hard to find Jesus. No one could fault their effort, but Jesus had a very hard word for them. He said that they did not follow Him because of the miraculous signs that were to point people to Him, the Prophet-King, rather they followed because He had fed them. These people followed Jesus not to see their lives change or to submit to Him as Lord, but because they wanted Him to meet their needs (John 6:16-27).

I understand that many people come to Jesus to have needs met. They may have damaged their life on addictions and immorality. Their marriage may be failing, or they recognize that their lives have no meaning. Jesus promises to meet our needs (Philippians 4:19), and He does. However, He has not come just to be "the warehouse clerk in the sky," He has come to be Lord. In fact, He cannot totally change our lives unless He is in the driver's seat. He must have access to every part of our lives for us to experience fullness of life. Jesus is not looking for those who determine truth by their own reasoning or feelings. He is not looking for people who want their needs met without committing their lives to Him. In fact, He cannot meet our deepest needs unless He is in control.

After these two encounters, John tells us that Jesus preached a very difficult sermon saying that a person only has part in Christ if he or she *eats His flesh* and *drinks His blood* (John 6:54). These comments obviously point to the broken body and shed blood of Jesus on the cross. However, the basic truth communicated in this passage is that believers will only make progress in becoming like Jesus, and in fulfilling their God-ordained destiny, when they put their faith in the person and work of the Lord Jesus Christ alone. He is the center of life and the only hope for humankind.

The results of Jesus' confrontations are predictable. Many of His "disciples" left Him. At this point, many modern-day pastors would have run after the people and been willing to soften the message to keep them. Jesus, however, did not budge. In fact, He turned to the twelve and said, *"You do not want to leave too, do you?"* (John 6:67). Peter responded, *"Lord, to whom shall we go? You have the words of eternal life*" (John 6:68). Peter is the kind of person Jesus had looked for and still looks for today. This is the person who says, "I don't always understand what You are saying and sometimes I don't like what You ask of me, but You are the only One with the words of eternal life. You are the only One who can make me fully alive!" Jesus could entrust Himself to Peter, and He can entrust Himself to people today who possess this kind of attitude.

During His lifetime, Jesus looked for those who would follow Him, no matter what He asked them to do, regardless of their circumstances. The reason is that Jesus could not entrust the task of taking the Gospel to the ends of the earth to those with a questionable commitment to Him and His purpose. Those with a half-hearted commitment may never get around to taking the Gospel to others. They may have a soft spot in their heart for Jesus and His work, but they do not go to bed thinking how they will reach the lost, and get up determined to do what God wants them to do. They will not relegate their personal agenda to a secondary position in order to advance His Kingdom. The writer of Second Chronicles gave this pitiful obituary of King Rehoboam: *"He did evil because he had not set his heart on seeking the Lord"* (2 Chronicles 12:14).

Second, Jesus knew that believers would have trouble on the earth, and He knew that semi-committed people would wilt when they experienced trouble (John 16:33). This trouble can come in the form of persecution, physical and financial problems, or the personal sacrifices of ministering to difficult people or going to hard places. It can also come as counsel from friends seeking to assist you to avoid "trouble." They may think that you are a bit overboard in your commitment. They genuinely have your best interests at heart, but think you are getting too radical. However, remember the world is made up of people whose relationship with God is severed. Their perspective is twisted. Their arguments can be quite persuasive, and if we are not fully committed to Kingdom living, these pressures will cause us to back off. Jesus knew that the faint of heart would back off, in order to take the pressure off their situation.

Unfortunately in our day, at least in the U.S., some of the worldly rejection might come from those in churches who claim to be followers of Christ. Kerry and I have had times when fellow believers have tried to discourage us from ministering in dangerous places. They were well meaning, but we had to say, "God has called us." We are open to counsel from our board and family when we do go to dangerous places, but we are committed to going wherever God calls us. We pray that if He does not want us to go, He will cancel trips.

We have had two trips canceled, where we would have been in serious danger had we gone. I will tell you about one of them. We were scheduled to go to India in November 2008. Many months prior to our trip, our Indian leadership team asked us not to come because of the political climate leading up to their election. I remember being disappointed. On the 26th of November, we watched a live newscast via the Internet, of the devastation caused in Mumbai by terrorists. We found out later that the terrorist had been looking for those with British and U.S. passports. We would have been traveling into Mumbai from another location in Maharashtra, to fly to the U.S. while the attacks were taking place. We believe that God protected us from potential danger.

Jesus also knew that He and His Church have an enemy wanting to stop the Church's advance. Sometimes Satan inspires the world to react more vehemently than "normal." When this resistance comes, it can get discouraging. Those who are half-hearted will not plow through.

The original disciples experienced imprisonment, rejection, and martyrdom, yet they kept going. Paul was abused in many ways, and yet he did not give up. In our day, courageous pastors spend years in China's prisons. After they serve their terms and are released from prison, they begin to minister to their people again. Many of them have been to prison multiple times. Why? Because they have determined to live to serve Christ, and their purpose on earth is to advance the Kingdom of God, no matter what comes their way. The results are staggering. According to a Chinese pastor, my wife and I heard that there are now 70 million believers in China. The Kingdom goes forth through a committed Church, undeterred by adversity. Jesus made it clear that it was costly to follow Him.

COMMIT FULLY TO CHRIST

Why would we want to fully commit ourselves to Christ? Jesus answers this question when He says:

> *Whoever wants to be my disciple must deny themselves and take up their cross daily and follow me. For whoever wants to save their life will lose it, but whoever loses their life for me will save it. What good is it for someone to gain the whole world, and yet lose or forfeit their very self?* (Luke 9:23-25)

What could Jesus be talking about? This two verses seem like double talk. However, when we begin to realize that Jesus used two Greek words that have been translated "life" in English, it begins to make sense. The life that Jesus tells us to lose is the Greek word *psyche,* from where we get our word psychology. It is the life that we can produce by our own intellect, emotions, and will—the life that humans can produce, apart from God; the life humankind has produced since the sin of Adam and Eve. Jesus says that if you give up *psyche,* then He will give us *zoe* life. *Zoe* is the life of God. We see this life demonstrated in the life of the Lord Jesus Christ. He told us that if we give up the life we can produce, He will manifest His life in us.

When Jesus asked them, *"What good is it for a man to gain the whole world...,"* He acknowledges that humans can accomplish many things here on earth. Remember the great accomplishments of agriculture, music, and manufacturing that we discussed from Genesis 4? In our day, humankind has developed means of transportation that can take us to the far corners of the earth in a short amount of time, and even into space above the earth. We have beautiful buildings, smart phones, and super computers that make our lives easier and more enjoyable. We observe athletic achievements that amaze us.

Unfortunately, humans cannot change their character, so Jesus says, "What will you gain if you get all these things but lose your soul?" Is it worth losing what you were created to be and to lose the eternal home where you were meant to live? Jesus asks, *"What good is it...."* Those who have chosen to follow hard after Jesus say, "It is *no* good!"

Therefore, in essence, Jesus is saying, give up what you can produce and take up your cross (whatever comes your way as a result of your obedience to God), and follow Him daily. In other words, live every moment of every day the way He wants you to live. You will gain *zoe!* You will be fully alive!

FATHER REALLY DOES KNOW BEST!

As we contemplate the decision to give our lives to Jesus, we may wonder, *Does God really know what's best for me?* In the United States, we pride ourselves on our "rugged individualism." No one tells us what to do. We have been continually told that we know what is best for us. We have been told to "follow your heart." In spite of this, America has extremely high divorce rates, violence impacts every sector of society, and a rising number of people are prescribed anti-depressants.[2]

Moving to the global scene, tensions in many parts of the world produced two World Wars in the past 100 years, and there are continuing conflicts in Iraq and Afghanistan, as well as internal conflicts throughout Africa and between Russia and the people of Ukraine. In 2011, citizens violently fought against their own governments producing the "Arab Spring," that enabled terrorists to overthrow evil dictators and claim leadership of their nations.[3] Acts of terror make the evening news broadcasts several times per week.

In September 2013, a dear friend of mine lost his mother and both of his children when two suicide bombers blew themselves up outside a church in Peshawar, Pakistan, leaving at least 100 dead and many more injured. In addition, we see millions living in poverty while others live in luxury. Humankind has not solved the overwhelming problems plaguing people worldwide. We have not made the world a better place.

PROMISES DELIVERED!

Jesus has asked us to make an extreme commitment to Him, and He has made many promises—but can He deliver what He has promised? John has anticipated that his readers will have this very question, so he dedicates much of his Gospel to declaring the greatness of Jesus. We will now take a look at the greatness of the Lord Jesus Christ.[4] Let us take some time to talk about Jesus and what He provides for us. He not only makes promises, He delivers!

He is God! When we buy an appliance, the manual tells us that it will work best when used as instructed. The manufacturer of the product knows what the product has been built to do. Therefore, we must assume that our Creator knows what will make for the most satisfying and fulfilling life—as He designed us with a purpose. In the first chapter of John's Gospel, he tells us that Jesus was there in the beginning with God, that He is God, and that He created everything (John 1:1-3). He knows how we function best. He knows what will make us function at the optimum level. He knows what will make us fully alive. Do we want to make decisions impacted by our sin nature, or do we want to listen to the One who created us?

A few years ago, I was talking with a friend who said, "I'm doing what I was created to do!" My wife and I feel the same way. If we listen to our Creator, Jesus, we can all move into that place.

Jesus' perfect life enlightens. As we continue in the first chapter of John, John tells us that Jesus had life in Him, which enlightens people. The life that Jesus lived is the life of God, which enabled Him to live perfectly, even when He lived on earth. We observe what abundant living looks like when we look at the life of Jesus Christ. Everyone, even those who do not believe that Jesus is Lord and Creator, recognizes the greatness of His life. Muslims see Him as a prophet of God, Hindus see Him as one of their millions of gods, and many who say they do not believe in any religion see Him as a great moral teacher. A number of years ago, I heard an actor, famous at the time, tell about his program to enhance life. As he espoused some New Age-type philosophy, he quoted Jesus Christ. This man, not a genuine follower of Jesus Christ, quoted Him in order to add authority to his philosophy of life.

Jesus' life enlightens us in such a way that we see what life can be. Although we have fallen short, we see our own potential, because everyone who has been born again has the ability to become like Jesus. Jesus tells us that those who obey the Word *"...will know the truth, and the truth will set you free"* (John 8:32). The freedom we gain is the freedom to become all that God created us to be.

Jesus is the only way to new life. During a discussion with some Pharisees (John 9:40–10:21), Jesus told them that there was only one way that people could gain entrance into the Kingdom. He told them that He was the way when He said, *"I am the gate for the sheep"* (John 10:7). No one else can forgive our sins, deliver us from shame, and set us on the path God intended for us. Jesus said that the Father had given Him the ability to determine who would have life. It is those who believe in Him who will *"cross over from death to life"* (John 5:19-24). Peter told those who took him into custody, *"there is no other name under heaven given to mankind by which we must be saved"* (Acts 4:12). Therefore, if we want to start over, there is only one place we can go. Jesus is the Source of our salvation!

Nick Pirovolos was a thug. He had been in prison for his activities, and to this day has a crease in his skull where a bullet nearly killed him. While in prison, Nick met someone who told him that Jesus could make him a new person. Initially he resisted, but eventually, he came to know Jesus Christ. He was released from prison and today helps inmates in prisons all over the southern part of the U.S.[5] Jesus changes people!

Jesus is the perfect guide. There are three key ways Jesus guides us:

1. *He is the Word (logos* in Greek) *of God (John 1:1,14)*. The Word of God is the truth concerning how we should live. The fact that Jesus is the Word of God suggests that the truth about life resides in Him. Because truth resides in Him and emanates from Him, He created us to live the same way. He guides us by revealing the Word of God to us through both His earthly teaching and by the written Word of God contained in the Old and New Testaments.

2. *He is the light (John 8:12, John 1:4)*. Because Jesus is the Word of God and because He has life in Him, His life enlightens people. If you do not understand how to live for God, look at the life of Jesus and you will find the answer.

3. *He is the Good Shepherd (John 10:11,14)*. As we submit to Him, He will guide us in every aspect of our lives, from *"green pastures"* to *"the valley of the shadow of death"* (Psalm 23). He knows what is best for the world, and He knows what is best for us as individuals. He guides us through the indwelling Holy Spirit.

After I graduated from college, I had a decision to make between two attractive choices. I had been accepted to attend Asbury Theological Seminary, an excellent seminary located near Lexington, Kentucky, and I had been asked to go to State College, Pennsylvania and receive discipleship training from a well-known campus ministry. In many ways, Asbury seemed like the logical choice because I was heading toward pastoral ministry. However, in my heart, I wanted to move to State College. I was at a place where I needed to make a decision.

I went to the Sunday school room of the church I attended and sought the Lord. I prayed and read the Scripture. As I read, I came to Psalm 20:4, which says, *"May he give you the desire of your heart and make all your plans succeed."* This Scripture caught my eye. I thought that God was telling me that He had placed moving to State College on my heart, and that was what He wanted me to do. As I kept reading, I read Psalm 21:2, which told me, *"You have granted him his heart's desire and have not withheld the request of his lips."* This convinced me that I should go to State College.

I obeyed what I believed the Lord was telling me, not knowing what was ahead. When I moved to State College, I was not able to get a job in the field I had been trained in. I took a menial job, and spent two years in training and then moved to another campus to start a campus ministry. Not long after I moved, I met Reverend Reynold Waltimyer, whom I mentioned earlier. I began to help him in his small church, where he gave me opportunities to teach and preach. He gave me opportunities to shadow him in ministry and serve on the church leadership team. He effectively mentored me for pastoral ministry.

A couple of years later, God called me to pastor a very small church nearby. The church I served was 30 minutes from Williamsport, Pennsylvania, where I met a wonderful young Child Evangelism County Director on a blind date. She became my wife six months later! God knows the future and He knows what is best for us, even when it does not make sense to our human reasoning. By the way, I did attend seminary, sixteen years later.

Jesus can make dead places alive. Jesus told His followers that He was (and is) *"the resurrection and the life"* (John 11:25). Jesus made this remarkable statement to Martha, sister of Lazarus, right before He raised Lazarus from the dead. Lazarus had been rotting in the grave for four days when Jesus arrived, but as Jesus ministered at the tomb that day, this dead man came to life!

Jesus' statement about being the resurrection and the life includes more than the raising of Lazarus. Paul tells us that because Jesus rose from the dead, we can walk in newness of life (Romans 6:4-6).

This is exactly what happens in our lives when we are born again. We were spiritually dead, separated from God, but when Jesus forgives our sins and comes into our lives, we come alive. The Spirit of God enters our lives, opening a connection with God, and energizing us with an infusion of the life of Jesus. Spiritually, we are raised from the dead. After we are born again, we come to life—body, soul, and spirit.

Jesus changes us the moment He comes into our lives. However, He never stops changing us. We are in process. There are areas of our lives that are still not quite alive by Jesus' standards. We might say that these areas are dead, or at least on life-support. Jesus wants to change these areas. He wisely chooses which areas need to change, and in which order He will work on them. As He touches us with His resurrection life, the areas that He is changing will become more like He desires them to be. The resurrection power of Jesus continually moves us from death to life.

In September 2013, Kerry and I traveled to India. One of the first "official" ministries that we engaged in was to speak at a pastors' meeting. As I prayed about this meeting, I felt that I should speak on overcoming discouragement. After the meeting a young pastor told me that he had become so discouraged that he wanted to quit the ministry. God did something in his heart that day, and he had come to peace with his calling and continuing in the ministry. There had been a dead place in his life that resurrected that day! God does such a powerful work in our lives when we allow Him. In addition to the wonderful things that Jesus does in our lives while we live on earth, the Scriptures make it clear that those who believe in Jesus will some-day spend eternity with God. This is the ultimate resurrection.

WHAT DOES COMMITMENT MEAN?

Jesus told His followers that *"unless a kernel of wheat falls to the ground and dies, it remains only a single seed. But if it dies, it produces many seeds"* (John 12:24). This is dying to the *psyche* life, the one that we can produce on our own. It means that if we give our entire life to Him, telling Him that we want to live the life He wants us to live, we will accomplish eternally valuable things.

The following are three key aspects of our lives that are affected when we give ourselves fully to Him:

1. *We surrender the "big" areas of our lives*—our *psyche* life for His *zoe* life including who we will marry,[6] what kind of career we will pursue, and where we will work.

2. *We will obey Him as He gives us day-to-day direction.* As we allow God to be in control of the major decision areas, we will also want to learn to obey as He speaks to us daily through His Word, and as we listen to Him in prayer. There will be times when God will show us something to do that is not on our to-do list for that day. For example, my wife and I recently felt led to visit a certain church. We have ministered there many times, but the Lord di-rected us to attend, even though we were not speaking. As we were greeting people, one of the men in the church handed me a large wad of bills. There were twenty-nine $20 bills there! He said that when he saw us, He felt that the Lord told him to give this money to us. Although our ministry had been struggling financially, we did not go there for this reason, or even have any expectations

that God would supply funds for us. God had directed us there that day so we could enjoy a great worship service and message and so He could bring a blessing to us through an obedient servant.

3. *We will allow God to change areas in our life*. He changes us so we can have freedom to be all that God intended. We will talk about his topic in the next chapter.

Are you ready to begin this new life? Have you ever received Jesus Christ into your life and been born again? If not, I encourage you to trust Him today. Ask Him to forgive your sins, come into your life, and make you a new person. Then, tell Him that you are turning your whole life over to Him. Thank Him for making you a new person, and for the life He has designed especially for you.

Perhaps you have previously received Jesus Christ into your life, but have not turned everything over to Him. Ask Him to forgive you for holding back part of your life from Him. (Be specific about the areas and sins that you have held onto.) Tell Him that from now on, He has control of your whole life.

Congratulations! You have just put yourself in a position to live the life God desires, which is to be fully alive!

ENDNOTES

1. My translation.

2. Please no emails. I am not suggesting that counseling and medications are not needed at times. I have two friends who are effective Christian counselors. I mention this to show that something is lacking in our society.

3. Unfortunately for Christians, radical Muslims have taken over many of these nations and an already bad situation for them has gotten

much worse, as the radicals seek to rid their nations of Christians (and anyone else) who will hinder them from instituting Islamic law, which they believe will bring paradise on earth.

4. Although we do not have time to deal with it here, the Scriptures make it clear that we have only one God (Deuteronomy 6:4). However, John 1:1 tells us that Jesus was in the beginning, before the creation existed and participated in the creation. Acts 5:1-5 calls the Holy Spirit, God. Therefore, the only conclusion we can come to is that in a way that is too difficult for us to understand, God is One, but exists in three equal Persons. Therefore, whatever characteristic we find in one member of the Godhead (Father, Son, or Holy Spirit) is also found in the other two.

5. Read Nick's story in *Too Mean to Die* by Nick Pirovolos with William Proctor (Wheaton, IL: Living Books, Tyndale House, 2009).

6. If you are already married, you are meant to be married to the person you are currently married to.

CHAPTER NINE

Allow God to
Remove Hindrances

In 1998, I resigned from the church my wife and I had led for eight and a half years. We didn't know what we were going to do, but we felt led to leave the church, and believed we would be training Christian leaders. We had lived in a church parsonage, so we needed to find a place to live. We began looking for homes in our price range. One of the houses we looked at had major problems with upstairs floor boards, which would have required major repairs. Sometime later, we looked at a townhouse that seemed to be well built and looked promising, until we went to the basement. There was moisture and the kind of critters that live on moist walls. Although both of these homes fell within our price range, we did not want to live in them.[1] We believed they would not have enabled us to do all that God had called us to do in raising our children and exercising hospitality for ministry. We could have lived in them, but we would have been hindered. Sometimes there are areas of our life that hinder God from giving us the full life that He wants to give us— hindering him from using us like He would like to. Although we chose to get a different home to find what we felt we needed, God is fully able to remove those things that hinder us from following Him, and give us the fullness of life that He desires to give. So, let's let Him remove anything that hinders us.

We have been examining Jesus' statements recorded in John 15:1-8 (more about this in Chapter 10). Verse 4 says, *"Remain in me, as I also remain in you...."* In his commentary on the Gospel of John, theologian Leon Morris says, "Jesus means that the disciples should live such lives that He will continue to abide in them."[2] Morris is not saying that Jesus totally leaves a person with the result that they are no longer a believer. Rather, he means that believers should live in such a way that Jesus will feel welcomed to enter their lives and take control of them.

We have already discussed the first way that we remain in Him. We begin to remain in Him when we *give our lives totally to Him* as we discussed in the previous chapter. In this chapter, we will discuss the need to allow Jesus to remove those habits and sins that hinder Him from making us what He desires.

A few years ago, one of our ministry's board members was struggling physically. As doctors examined him, they found plaque buildup in an artery that slowed the flow of blood in his system. They quickly made plans to push the plaque out using angioplasty, and insert a stint in the artery to prevent further plaque buildup.

When you and I were born again, the Spirit of Christ came to live in our spirit. However, we come into this new life carrying baggage in the form of sin and bad habits that we committed prior to coming to Jesus. These old ways of living act like plaque in the blood stream, which hinders the full manifestation of the life of Jesus in our lives. The writer of Hebrews[3] discusses this important subject. Let's take a look at Hebrews 10:32–12:3. I suggest that you read the entire passage before you continue reading, in order to understand the entire passage, where we reference specific verses from the following passage.

At the end of Chapter 10, Paul talks about a time in the life of these believers when they endured persecution and the confiscation of their property, while they gladly stood with those imprisoned for their faith (Hebrews 10:33-34). However, since Paul had to remind them of those early days, we assume that they no longer endured such difficulty with their previous tenacity. Paul warned them not to *"throw away your confidence"* (Hebrews 10:35) because *"we are not of those who shrink back"* (Hebrews 10:39). He wants his readers to understand that believers should not allow their circumstances to hinder them from moving forward into the purposes of God.

Paul immediately begins to tell them about a group of people who experienced difficulty in their lives, and remained faithful until the end of their lives (Hebrews 11). He talks of men like Enoch who was translated directly to heaven because of his righteousness, Noah, Abraham, Joseph, and Moses. Later he mentions some others we may not know as well. We may even ask why some of them have been included: Rahab, the prostitute; Barak, who would not go into battle without the prophetess, Deborah, by his side; and Jepthah, whose character was questionable. He says that these and others remained faithful to the end, *"yet none of them received what had been promised"* (Hebrews 11:39; see also 11:13). In other words, it was not their success and/or blessing that kept them going, but their faith.

As I have pondered this passage in Hebrews, it seemed to me that many of them saw God fulfill many promises. Why then would Paul say that none of them received what had been promised? I believe that Paul meant that none of these Old Testament heroes saw the coming of the Prophet-King, who had been promised throughout the pages of the Old Testament; so, none of them had the privilege of living by the continual power of the indwelling Holy Spirit 24/7. These believers remained faithful until death, even though they did not possess the power for living, experienced by New Testament believers.

Later, Paul says, *"we are surrounded by such a great cloud of witnesses"* (Hebrews 12:1) who demonstrate to us that we can remain faithful to God, no matter what our circumstances may be. In light of those who have already endured to the end, he exhorts them—and us—to *"throw off everything that hinders and the sin that so easily entangles. And let us run with perseverance the race marked out for us"* (12:1). In essence Paul said, "If there is spiritual plaque in your life, then let God push it out. If the plaque can be removed, then the life of Jesus will become evident in every part of our lives."

Imagine, for a moment, what it would be like to have Jesus living His life through us. Paul prays that the believers in the church at Ephesus would have this very experience. Let's see what Paul tells them will happen if Jesus lives in them. (Please read Ephesians 3:12-21.)

1. Paul prays that the Holy Spirit would gain more strength in the believers' lives so that Christ would live in them. When the Holy Spirit gains control of a believer's life (as the person commits fully to Jesus and allows Him to remove hindrances from fully experiencing His life), Jesus will be able to live His life more fully in the believer.

2. Paul then tells his readers that when Jesus is firmly in charge of their lives, the foundation of their lives will be love. This implies that we will have greater contact with other parts of the Body of Christ. This is important. Jesus is too big to reveal Himself fully to one part of the Body of Christ. As a result, He gives different burdens to different groups. For example, helping the poor, Salvation Army; missions and evangelism, the Assemblies of God and Baptists; life in the Word, Evangelicals; and how to move in the Holy Spirit, Pentecostal and Charismatics. The groups mentioned focus upon these specific areas (and others)

because God has given them this focus. As we fellowship with one another across denominational lines, we benefit from each other's strengths, and we all come to a greater understanding of how wide, long, high, and deep God's love is. We all grow.

3. Paul then says that when this happens, we will be filled to all the fullness of God.

4. The end result is that we will live life beyond our wildest dreams. This is the life He planned for us since creation. When we live like this, we are *fully alive!*

Does this sound like the kind of life you would like to live? Is this the kind of life worth pursuing, no matter the cost?

As I write this chapter, the 2014 Winter Olympics are about to begin. I love watching the amazing feats the athletes perform. I also enjoy the biographical information provided about the athletes. Many of these Olympians have sacrificed nearly everything in order to train and gain the skills necessary to make the national team or to stand on the podium after they have won a medal. They change what they eat, live according to regimented schedules, and spend time gaining strength and skills. As they continue training, their coaches point out habits that hinder their quest for gold. I am challenged by their commitment, because I find that these athletes are willing to sacrifice nearly everything for a piece of metal, and the prestige that goes with it. Unfortunately, I find that many believers are unwilling to make the same commitment in order to expand the Kingdom of God.

FOUR HINDRANCES

In the remainder of the chapter, we will discuss four areas that could hinder us in our quest to live life at its fullest, and how we can push those hindrances out of our lives, with God's help. We will be examining sin, strongholds, demonic strongholds, and unforgiveness.

I. SIN

When we think of sin, certain activities often come to mind.[4] The actions we often think of are sexual impurity, stealing, lying, and the like. As we focus on these sins, some people think God actually wants our lives to be miserable or boring. The opposite is the case. The word sin means "missing the mark." The idea pictures someone shooting an arrow and missing the target. When we engage in sin of any kind, we miss the mark God has set for us, which is to be fully alive.

Therefore, when God points out sin in our lives, He is showing us areas that hinder us from living the ultimate life. He is like a batting coach in baseball who studies a player's swing and makes suggestions to help the player improve his batting average. God points out sin because He knows that these flaws are holding us back. He wants us to do better. How do we get rid of activities that cause us to miss the mark?

- *Ask God to point out actions and attitudes in your life that hinder you from experiencing life at its fullest* (see David's prayer recorded in Psalm 51). If you have given your life completely to Jesus, you want to be everything He created you to be, so why not ask Him to point out the things in your life that are "missing the mark."

- As God shows these areas to you, *confess them and repent of the sin.* After God points out an area, your first response should be to confess the activity as sin. To confess means "to say the same thing as." In other words, when we confess our sin, we agree with God that what we are doing is robbing us of the life He wants to give us. Biblical confession includes repentance. The word *repent* literally means "to change our mind about something." This means that anything God shows us is wrong, even if we thought it was okay, we will change our mind to agree with God's thinking. When our mind has changed, then our activities should change as well. This is true biblical repentance.

David expresses how repentance works. He asks, *"How can a young person stay on the path of purity? By living according to your word."* He then says, *"I have hidden your word in my heart that I might not sin against you"* (Psalm 119:9,11). He says that he knows that if he hides God's Word in his heart, his mind will change, and thus his actions will line up with the will of God.

Note that John gives a wonderful promise when he tells us to confess our sin. He says, *"If we confess our sins, he is faithful and just and will forgive us our sins and purify us from all unrighteousness"* (1 John 1:9). He says that when we confess our sins—genuinely confess, with a repentant heart,[5] God will purify us from our sin. Sometimes, we must keep confessing repeated sins until we gain victory in a specific area of our lives, just like we need to wash our hands several times if we have been repairing a car. I had a persistent area like that, early in my walk with the Lord. As I would confess the sin, I didn't think that anything had changed, until one day. I realized then, that the sin was no longer part of my life. God had given victory. I was more alive than I had been, before I sought God to change me.

- *Seek God for direction to overcome your sin.* God knows what it will take to overcome a particular sin in your life. He may ask you to stay away from certain places, or change your viewing habits. He may ask you to memorize a Scripture that will help you in the repentance process. He may ask you to make yourself accountable to someone, or to seek Christian counseling or a support group. Do whatever He asks you to do! There are times when our sinful habits want to hang on. We may try everything mentioned, and the sin continues to persist. Let's discuss this further, and see what we can do.

2. STRONGHOLDS

A stronghold is an area of our lives where sin has become so entrenched that it seems we cannot break free from it. These sins have become so entwined with our personality that we seem doomed to failure the rest of our lives.

We will deal with some strongholds the same way we dealt with sin in the previous section. But with strongholds, we need to persist until the victory comes. In the case of most strongholds, however, we may need help from others. It is good to go to a trusted spiritual leader for prayer and assistance. The leader may have overcome the same stronghold, or may identify the source of your problem like a good batting coach. We will discuss two types of strongholds and talk about how we can get free.

A. Informational Strongholds

It was an event that would impact my life and the life of my family for twenty-five years. The influence was so subtle that I did not know it existed. I went into the garage to help my dad with a project. I failed to complete the task successfully. Dad angrily responded, "Boy, you can't do anything right!" I was devastated. Although the initial feelings vanished, the words went deep into my soul and secretly distorted my perceptions of myself. Deep inside I believed that I couldn't "do anything right!" I began to believe that I was only acceptable when I performed well, but I rarely believed that I had. Even when I received an A on a paper in seminary, I frequently did not believe it was really that good. As a result, anger lurked beneath the surface of my life, waiting for opportunities to manifest and causing me to erupt in irrational ways. Words have power. That one sentence spoken to me by my dad (I frankly do not know if he really meant these words or just spoke in frustration) held me captive for decades. Fortunately, God can set us free from negative words.

Solomon tells us that *"the tongue has the power of life and death"* (Proverbs 18:21). Our words have the power to motivate people to reach their God-ordained destiny, or they can discourage them from pursuing what will benefit their lives.[6]

Words can produce death in our lives. Cruel words, the lies of the enemy, separate us from the life of God, and imprison us when we believe they are true. They are words of death. Many people have made bad decisions that negatively impacted their lives, because they based their life on the cruel words of a miserable or angry person.

> For though we live in the world, we do not wage war as the world does. The weapons we fight with are not the weapons of the world. On the contrary, they have divine power to **demolish strongholds.** We demolish arguments and every pretension that sets itself up against the knowledge of God, and we take captive every thought to make it obedient to Christ (2 Corinthians 10:3-5).

Paul's discussion of words, in the context of teaching on spiritual warfare, demonstrates that our mind is a battlefield. Pretensions are insights that seem logical but do not line up with the Scriptures. They become ungodly mindsets that influence the way we live, often with tragic results.

However, it can get even worse. Arguments occur when our pretensions become so entrenched that we defend the action as appropriate for ourselves and others. For instance, people may become so convinced of the benefits of abortion that they participate in marches, fight for legislation, and seek to persuade women to have an abortion. I call these arguments and pretensions "informational strongholds."

These strongholds can cause us to reject the truth of God because we have become convinced that untruth is truth. They keep us from confession and repentance. The lie that I believed caused me to have difficulty believing that good things could happen to me, or believing that God could use me in a significant way.

How can we overcome this kind of stronghold? The writer of Hebrews tells us that the Word of God penetrates deep into our being, dividing even between our soul and spirit (Hebrews 4:12). Dr. Ed Silvoso tells us that this means that the Word of God penetrates so deeply into our being that it exposes the arguments of our human reasoning and establishes the truth in our human spirit. The truth of God replaces the enemy's lie, and we gain freedom that allows us to live as God desires.[7]

In my case, God spoke to me from Romans 8:15, where Paul declares that we can cry out to God, calling Him *"Abba"* (Daddy, Father). As this truth sunk into my being, I realized that God loves me because I am His son, John. He wants me to succeed, but His love does not depend on my performance.

Many people live their lives based upon false understandings that, if left unchecked, will become strongholds. I have listed a few:

1. "I will never amount to anything."

2. "God can't forgive me of_____."

3. "God can't use me after what I have done."

4. "No one really likes me."

5. "No one could ever love me."

Our unbiblical beliefs can become *word curses*. A word curse is an unbiblical belief that has the power to keep us from fulfilling the purposes of God. When we believe that a lie is truth, we order our lives to make the lie become reality. Some call this a self-fulfilling prophecy. If we believe that we will never amount to anything, we may not apply for a promotion or pursue a ministry because we believe we will not be considered. We sabotage our lives, dooming ourselves to mediocrity or failure.

How do we overcome informational strongholds? Ask the Lord to identify any informational strongholds in your life. Here are some questions that may help you identify them:

1. Do I make negative or unbiblical statements, especially when I am discouraged? What are they?

2. When I hear biblical truths, do I find myself thinking: *This must mean someone or something else.*

3. Ask a friend if he or she sees any unbiblical beliefs in your life.

Once you have identified the unbiblical belief in your life, ask the Lord to give you a personal Scripture that explains God's truth about the subject you have falsely believed. Then ask Him to eradicate the lie of the enemy and embed His truth in your spirit. Meditate upon the Scripture until God changes your thinking in this area.

B. Soul Ties

Those engaging in sexual sin form ungodly "soul ties." Paul says that sexual sin is unique because it is sin against our bodies (1 Corinthians 6:18-20). This statement raises questions, because other sins such as drugs, alcoholism, and gluttony impact the body. Therefore, we must conclude that sexual immorality must sin against our body in a unique way. Dr. Freda McKissic Bush and Dr. Joe McIlhaney Jr. have reported through medical research that powerful chemicals are released in our brain during sex. For women, it is oxytocin and for men vasopressin. These chemicals cause a man and woman to bond to each other. In addition, both men and women get addictive doses of dopamine during a sexual encounter. These chemicals bond couples who are having a sexual relationship. This is great for those wanting a lifelong relationship. However, this is not good for those engaging in casual sex. McIlhaney and Bush say that when people tear away from relationships, by going from partner to partner, that the brain resists the deep emotional levels needed for marriage because they have rejected the bonding created by these God-given chemicals. Casual sex sins against our body.[8]

We have seen in our ministry, that when people engage in sexual immorality, they sin against their bodies in another way. Those who engage in sexual sin develop an emotional bond, which may not go away. We have seen believers, who sinned sexually before conversion, unable to get previous partners out of their minds during sex with their spouses. One man told me this was like having three people in bed when he was with his wife. However, when a person confesses this sin, he is able take a place of authority, in Jesus, and break the soul tie. After confessing their sin and repenting, they can say, "In the name of the Lord Jesus Christ, I break this soul tie." We have seen amazing transformation come with this simple, authoritative prayer. The man who felt there were three in his bed told me that God fully delivered him after this simple prayer.

3. Demonic Strongholds

There are times when our sin opens the door for our enemy, Satan, to gain some control in our lives. This often takes the form of some type of demonic bondage. This has become a debated subject because many of our Bible translations talk about "demon possessed." This implies that the demon has gained complete control of the person. Although in some instances, unbelievers may be completely controlled, believers have been purchased by the blood of the Lord Jesus Christ and are owned by Him. Therefore, *Christians cannot be possessed or owned by a demon*. Instead of "demon possessed," the translators would have been more accurate to translate the word as "demonized." When a person is demonized, the spirit has some control, but not full control. The amount of control will vary from person to person. Demonization comes when a person opens the door for a spirit to gain influence in his or her life by engaging in certain sins, worshiping false gods or participating in the occult. For a believer, it may be sin committed prior to conversion that was not dealt with, or sin committed after the person has come to Christ.

Some may wonder where we get such teaching. I will attempt, in the limited space that I have in this book, to address the subject. However, I encourage you to get one of the many good books on this subject. *Breaking Free to Your Destiny,* from KingdomQuest Ministries, is one of them.

On to the teaching. Let's look at Ephesians 4:26-27. Paul tells His readers, *"In your anger do not sin: Do not let the sun go down while you are still angry, and do not give the devil a foothold."* He tells his readers that if they do not deal with their anger, they may cross a line that gives the devil a foothold. The word foothold is the Greek word *topos,* meaning a piece of land. Therefore, we can say that a person can give ground to the enemy. In other words, we give him a base of operation in our lives where he can influence us, when we allow anger to fester too long.

It is my contention that Paul is using a broad principle here and applying it specifically to anger. In other words, we can give ground to the enemy through more sins than just anger. When a demonic spirit exercises control in a life, a stronghold sometimes develops. When a demonic stronghold forms in one's life, it must be broken by utilizing the authority that Jesus gives to us.

Before we get into specifics on how we can gain victory over a demonic stronghold in our lives, we must talk about our authority in Christ.

By what authority do we break the power of demonic spirits in our lives? (Again, space does not allow us to cover this topic in great detail. Please read Ephesians 1:15-2:10.) Paul begins his letter to the Ephesians by telling them about the wonderful blessings that God has provided to believers in Christ. Indeed, Paul tells them that God has given them every blessing they need in heaven, on earth, and in the realm of demons and angels, in order to walk in holiness.[9] These blessings include the love God has lavished upon believers, His sovereign rule over the events of their lives, and the indwelling power of the Holy Spirit.

Paul then prays that God would give them revelation in four areas:

1. The hope to which He has called us. This is the hope that we will live eternally with God in a state of perfection.

2. The riches of His glorious inheritance in the saints. Jesus' inheritance includes each person who has been born again, their growth in Christ, and their effective ministry. In other words, His inheritance is every aspect of the advance of His Kingdom in individuals and the Church as a whole.

3. The power available to us as believers. We have an enemy who is highly organized and whose cunning ways enable him to convincingly portray himself to be more formidable than he really is (Ephesians 6:10-13). In light of the fact that the enemy is organized and deceptive, Paul tells us that God has exceedingly great power available to believers. He compares this power to the power that *"he exerted when he raised Christ from the dead and seated him at his right hand in the heavenly realms, far above all rule and authority, power and dominion, and every name that is invoked, not only in the present age but also in the one to come"* (Ephesians 1:20-21). He says this to let us know the magnitude of His power available to us.

4. He seats us with Him at the place of authority (Ephesians 2:1-7). In these verses, Paul recounts the transformation that takes place in someone's life when the person receives Jesus Christ. He tells his readers that every person without Christ is spiritually dead and deserving of God's judgment.

At conversion, however, he receives forgiveness, is raised with Christ to newness of life and is seated with Christ in the place of authority, in the heavenly realms.

> *And God raised us up with Christ and seated us with him in the heavenly realms in Christ Jesus, in order that in the coming ages he might show the incomparable riches of his grace, expressed in his kindness to us in Christ Jesus* (Ephesians 2:6-7).

When Paul tells us that we sit with Christ in the heavenly realms, he does not mean that we sit with Him geographically. Rather, he says that we have the authority of the One sitting on the throne. He has placed us there so we can exercise authority over the enemy when he seeks to hinder us from fulfilling God's destiny in our lives. In Christ, we have the right to tell every demonic spirit who exercises control in our lives to leave! We exercise His power, not as one possessing that power, but as one with authority. We are like police officers. A police officer does not have the power to stop a truck or even a small car. However, the authority of the state stands behind him. When the police officer's hand goes up, we stop. When we tell demonic spirits to leave, they do so because we have the Father's power behind us. Therefore, when we take our place of authority, the demons must flee when we deal with them properly.

How do we expel demonic intruders? Consider seriously the following four ways:

1. We must confess our sin and repent of it. This means that we ask God to help us not commit this sin again. (Remember, our sin gave the ground to the enemy in the first place, so we must wipe the slate clean.)

2. We take our place of authority described. We say something like: "I now take my place of authority in the Lord Jesus Christ, victor over Satan and his demonic hosts." We must

understand that we are not just repeating words. We must believe the truth of the Word of God and exercise faith that God has commissioned us to do what we are doing.

3. **We take back the ground we have given to the enemy.** We do this by saying. "And now in the strong name of the Lord Jesus Christ, I take back all the ground I gave the enemy when I sinned, because I have repented and these sins are under the blood of the Lord Jesus Christ."

4. **We tell the demonic spirits who have lost their ground to leave in Jesus' name.** There are times when we may need help to expel spirits from our lives. In fact, I would recommend having a mature believer who understands spiritual warfare be present with you, as you seek to expel the enemy.

4. UNFORGIVENESS[10]

We have found that unforgiveness and bitterness are the number one reasons that believers do not experience freedom in Christ. A few years ago, we went to a meeting in a remote area in Gujarat, India. After the service, our translator asked if there were those who needed prayer. All the requests were for healing. Everyone we prayed for that night, including a baby who was near death, was healed—except one lady. She was obviously bitter and would not forgive family members for a real or perceived injustice. We believe God would have healed her if she had forgiven.

Our enemy, Satan, relishes it when we don't forgive, because our unforgiveness gives him a foothold in our lives. His foothold will hinder us from fulfilling our God-ordained destiny.

Webster defines forgiveness: *"To give up resentment against or the desire to punish; stop being angry with; pardon; to give up all claim to punish or exact penalty for and offense; to overlook, cancel, or remit a debt.*"[11] Someone else defines it as: *"Giving up my right to hurt you for hurting me."*

Jesus—our ultimate example—experienced great emotional pain when He was crucified, but He exercised forgiveness in its highest form while hanging on the cross. Isaiah said *"He was despised and rejected by men, a man of sorrows and familiar with suffering..."* (Isaiah 53:3). Yet Jesus forgave saying, *"Father forgive them for they do not know what they are doing"* (Luke 23:34). We might say, "But He was the Son of God!"

Another example of biblical forgiveness was Stephen. He was among seven men chosen to wait on tables and distribute food to the widows in the early Church. As he carried out his responsibilities, he exemplified the character of Christ and performed powerful signs and wonders.

When the religious leaders opposed him, he preached a powerful sermon about Jesus Christ, and challenged these leaders because they had rejected the Prophet/King. The leaders concluded that Stephen had committed blasphemy, and they stoned him to death. Stephen responded to their murderous act by praying for those who stoned him, just prior to his death, *"Lord, do not hold this sin against them"* (Acts 7:60).

Reasons why we need to forgive:

1. Jesus told us to forgive (Matthew 18:23-35). We read in His model prayer: *"Forgive us our debts, as we also have forgiven our debtors"* (Matthew 6:12). He implies that we can expect God to forgive us to the degree that we forgive others.

2. God forgives us (Psalm 103:2-3). Should we not follow His example?

3. We will receive answers to prayer (Mark 11:24-25): *"Therefore I tell you, whatever you ask for in prayer, believe that you*

have received it, and it will be yours. And when you stand praying, if you hold anything against anyone, forgive them, so that your Father in heaven may forgive you your sins."

4. It makes us like Jesus (Philippians 3:10; Luke 23:34).

5. It can release others (John 20:23): *"If you forgive anyone's sins, their sins are forgiven; if you do not forgive them, they are not forgiven."* Often when we forgive, God does a work in the person's life who wronged us. A friend of ours had been sexually molested by her father. When she forgave him, God did a work in his life, which resulted in him getting saved and making things right with her.

What forgiveness is NOT!

Sometimes we resist forgiving because we do not understand what forgiveness is and is not.

- Forgiveness is not approval of the wrong done.

- It is not excusing, denying, justifying, or pardoning the sin. (The person we forgive may still get expelled from school, lose a job, or be imprisoned.)

- It is not necessarily reconciliation. Although reconciliation should be a goal, it requires both persons. The other party may not want to reconcile.

- It is not pretending that the sin did not occur or pretending that we are not hurt.

- It is not forgetting.

What forgiveness IS:

Forgiveness is a process that may involve forgiving over and over until we know that it's complete. The following are some steps we must take to truly forgive. (We will need God's help to forgive. This may not be easy.)

- *We must surrender our case and our pain to the Lord.* As long as we hold on to our right to be angry and hold unforgiveness, we will never enjoy the freedom that forgiveness can bring.

- *We must choose to forgive.* Forgiveness is not a feeling, and it is not based on whether the person deserves it. It is an act of obedience that is followed by God's grace.

- *We must give up our right to be angry or to get even. We must ask God to forgive the person.* This can be a difficult step. We can sometimes forgive, but still want God to judge them. Remembering Jesus' words from the cross will help us.

- *We ask God to bless the person.* This sounds very difficult, but we have not completely forgiven until we really want God to bless them.

- *Do not repeat what the person did, unless it will help someone else.* If you feel it will help someone else you can relate the incident, but it is best not to use the person's name, if you can avoid it.

- *Ask God to forgive you for blaming Him for what happened to you.* God has never done anything wrong, but we sometimes blame Him for unpleasant events in our lives.

- *Determine to believe that all things work for good (Romans 8:28).* God often uses the greatest pain in our lives to produce our greatest ministry. Many counselors in drug rehab ministries are former addicts who have graduated from the program. Paul told believers at Corinth that God comforts us at our place of pain so that we can comfort others (2 Corinthians 1:3-4).

Pray a prayer like this: "Father, I forgive (<u>be specific</u>) for (<u>again be specific</u>). Father I ask you to forgive (<u>name of person being forgiven</u>) for what he/she has done. Now would you bless (<u>be specific</u>) in every way (<u>name of person be forgiven</u>) needs blessed. Save him/her (if he/she needs saved) and meet all other needs as well." If you do this, you are well on your way to freedom. Continue to pray this prayer until you have completely forgiven the person(s).

A few years ago, we were ministering in an Asian nation. A pastor came into our meeting who had been beaten and his church was burned because of a false allegation toward one of his parishioners. He came discouraged, fearful, and needing to forgive. My wife taught on forgiveness and gave the students time to be alone with God, in order to forgive. He was on his knees intently praying. He overcame his fear and went back to hold a service where his church had been, with a police escort that he was not expecting. The next week he came to our meeting. On the last night, we had a campfire that began with worship. This pastor ran to the middle of the gathering, dancing like David! His forgiveness had brought him great freedom! Our countenance even changes—when we forgive.

In Summary

As believers, we can allow "plaque" to build up in our spiritual lives. Review this chapter, and allow the Lord to point His finger at areas He would like to work on. Do whatever He asks in order to see the hindrances removed, so you can follow the great cloud of witnesses.

ENDNOTES

1. Not long after this, God showed us the townhouse that we live in now. It was and continues to be perfect for us.

2. Leon Morris, The New International Commentary on the New Testament—The Gospel According to John; F.F. Bruce, General Editor (Grand Rapids, MI: Wm. B. Eerdmans Publishing Co., 1971), 670.

3. There is some debate as to who wrote the Book of Hebrews. I believe the apostle Paul wrote Hebrews. Therefore, from now on when referencing Hebrews, I will credit Paul as the writer.

4. Often we focus on things that others do.

5. Some people confess sin to God because they feel guilty and are sad that they got caught, but they have no plan to change their activity. They are like the child who, when he disobeys, asks his parent for forgiveness, in order to cut down on punishment!

6. For a more detailed discussion of both the negative and positive impact of words, see *Breaking Free to Your Destiny* available from KingdomQuest Ministries at info@kquestministries.org.

7. Ed Silvoso, *That None Should Perish* (Ventura, CA: Regal Books, 1994), 166.

8. Cited in "Sexually Indulgent Now, Marriage Ruined Later" at www.cbn,com/cbnnews/healthscience/2010/Sexual   Indulgence;   accessed 10/6/2010.

9. This is implied when Paul tells them that they have the blessings in heavenly realm(s).

10. Much of the teaching in this chapter has been adapted from *Breaking Free to Your Destiny* by John and Kerry Shuey. Adapted with permission.

11. Webster's New World Dictionary of the American Language (Cleveland and New York: The World Publishing Company, 1962), 568.

CHAPTER TEN

Allow the Word to Live in You

In the last chapter, I told you about some houses that we did not want to purchase because of potentially costly flaws. We are so glad that we did not purchase either of them, and that we purchased our current home. Before we moved into our home, the previous owner had installed new carpets, finished a family room in the basement, and two friends painted the house for us. The previous owner took all of his furniture with him, so the house was clean, but empty. The house began to display our personality when our furniture was moved in and my wife began to use her decorating skills.

In John 15, Jesus told His disciples that they were clean because of the Word He had spoken to them (John 15:3). I believe He meant that they had been born again. They had been forgiven and were spiritually clean. In the last chapter, we talked about allowing the Lord to deal with issues in our lives that hinder Him from fully working in us.

When the hindrances have been removed, there is a void. Therefore, we need to allow Jesus to move spiritual furniture and decorations into our lives. After Jesus tells them to allow God to get rid of their hindrances, He tells them what to do next. He says, *"If you remain in me and my words remain in you..."* (John 15:7). We are to fill the void that is left when He removes our hindrances, by allowing the Word of God to live in us.

John frequently talked about the Word in his Gospel. He uses two Greek words thirty-six times, which we translate as "word." Some have taught that these two words, *logos* and *rhema,* possess different meanings. Although there are some subtle differences, I believe they are essentially the same. Let me illustrate this for you. In an earlier passage, Jesus says that His enemies would be judged for rejecting His words *(rhema)*. He then says that the word *(logos)* He spoke will condemn them (John 12:48). In this verse, these two Greek words are synonymous. I believe that both refer to the Bible, the Word of God. John uses a third word, *aletheia,* which has a similar meaning, twenty-five times in his Gospel. *Aletheia* is translated "truth," in English. In Jesus' prayer the night before He was crucified, Jesus asked His Father to sanctify His disciples. Jesus prays, *"Sanctify them by the truth; your word is truth"* (John 17:17). *Logos* and *aletheia* are used synonymously. Since John uses these three words sixty-three times in his Gospel, we must conclude that the Word, which is the truth, plays a key role in our lives as believers.

The Bible's Importance

Why is the Word of God, the Bible, so important? In Chapter 4, we discovered that Jesus is the One sent by God. Because Jesus is the Prophet-King, we can believe that His words are truth, because they are the words of God. Not only can we depend on the Gospels, but we can also depend on all of the Scripture. Paul, referring to the Old Testament Scriptures, says, *"All Scripture is God-breathed..."*

(2 Timothy 3:16). As Peter discusses the Old Testament, he says, *"For prophecy never had its origin in the human will, but prophets, though human, spoke from God as they were carried along by the Holy Spirit"* (2 Peter 1:21). Later in the same letter, Peter speaks of the writings of Paul and says, *"His letters contain some things that are hard to understand, which ignorant and unstable people distort, as they do the other Scriptures, to their own destruction"* (2 Peter 3:16). In saying this, Peter declares that the writings of Paul are Scripture.

In addition to these testimonies, the early Church went through a lengthy, prayerful process to determine which books and letters should be included in the New Testament.[1] We can be certain, as have believers through the ages, that the Bible is the Word of God, and it can be trusted as the source of truth.

JESUS' WORDS LIVING IN YOU

When we get off the airplane in India, we notice quite a difference. Not only are we in a different location, but we are in a different culture. Indians do things differently from Americans. For instance, my wife and I like to hold hands, wherever we are, to show our affection for each other. In the parts of India in which we travel, husbands and wives do not engage in any public display of affection. One evening we were having a nice meal at the home of one of the students who attended our seminar. We were taking photos, and I asked the pastor's wife, in a spirit of humor because I knew what her response would be, to put her arm around her husband. She said, shyly, that that would not be appropriate for her. Their culture is different.

When you and I came to Christ, we came into a new Kingdom, the Kingdom of God. We must unlearn some of our previous culture's traditions, the worldly way of life, and learn the culture of the Kingdom. John uses the Greek word *kosmos* sixty-nine times, when he describes the lifestyle and culture developed by humankind's godless reasoning and the inspiration of Satan. Because of our separation from God, we have codified non-truth into the religions and philosophies of life, into what theologians call "the world system." Because we lived in the world prior to coming to Christ, we accepted many of the world's habits and values. When we become believers, we must learn godly truth so we can walk in the principles of the Kingdom of God. As we discussed in the last chapter, some of these habits have become part of our lives and must be dislodged, through the grace of God.

Paul tells believers how they can become immersed in Kingdom-thinking, in his letter to the Ephesians. He tells his readers that when they came to Jesus Christ, they put off the sinful nature and put on a new nature (Ephesians 4:22,24). However, right between these verses he tells them, *"to be made new in the attitude of your minds"* (Ephesians 4:23). The putting off of the old nature and the putting on of the new nature happened when we were born again. Because the Holy Spirit has come to live in our lives, we are no longer separated from God. Therefore, we have put off the old nature, which entered humanity when they were no longer connected to God, and put on a new nature with new potential because we are connected to God. In order for us to fully experience the new nature, however, we must allow God to change the way we think. We must stop thinking like the world, and begin thinking like Jesus.[2]

The attitude of our minds does not change automatically. It does not even change automatically because we have changed our belief system. We all know people, and perhaps we have been one of them, who know all the right things to say in a Sunday school class or small group, but whose lives do not line up with what they say they believe.

A number of years ago, a friend and I led the youth group at our church. He went to visit one of the new students in the group. While at this home, the father of the student got out an extensive study he had done on biblical love. My friend said that while the man was sharing his discoveries about love, he acted in a very unloving way toward his family.

So, how do we change the way we think and the way we live? The truth must go from our mind to our heart (our spirit, which is the core of our being). John gives us some insight into how our thinking and actions can be changed. John tells us that one of the reasons he wrote this Gospel was so his readers would *"have life in his* [Jesus Christ's] *name"* (John 20:30-31). Whenever the name of Jesus or God is mentioned in Scripture, we observe a time when a servant of God has received a revelation of the nature of God that has moved from the person's mind to his or her heart or spirit. When this new revelation of God landed in the core of his or her life, the person's worldview changed. When a person's worldview changes—life changes.

When God provided the ram for Abraham to sacrifice in place of his son, he recognized that God was his Provider (Genesis 22). This revelation altered Abraham's life. When Moses threw the tree in the bitter waters, causing the water to become drinkable, he recognized that God is Healer (Exodus 15:22-27). Of course, Abraham and Moses had their minds changed, but the change went much deeper into their heart. Their lives had been changed. John wants his readers to have their lives altered through encountering Jesus in this way.

During our discussion on overcoming informational strongholds, we discussed how the principles of the Word of God go deep into our human spirit, the core of our being. As these principles go there, they expose the lies that we have believed, so that we can reject them and see them replaced with the truth of God. When we come to understand Scripture in this way, we call it revelation. As God gives us continuous revelation, our thinking changes and our mind is renewed. When our mind is renewed, we begin to think and act like Jesus.

THE IMPACT OF REVELATION

What is the impact of revelation in our lives? Revelation makes it possible for us to live life at its fullest. Here are some of the blessings of revelation:

Revelation enables us to know Jesus. On one occasion, Jesus discussed eternal life with some of His opponents. At one point, Jesus told them, *"You study the Scriptures diligently because you think that in them you have eternal life. These are the very Scriptures that testify of me"* (John 5:39). These religious leaders had missed Jesus—the subject of the Scriptures. Therefore, they missed eternal life. They had studied the Scriptures using their own ability to grasp the truth, but did not look to the Holy Spirit to enlighten them. When we allow the Holy Spirit to highlight the Scriptures, we receive revelation, which reveals Jesus in His glory and changes the way we think.

Revelation energizes our faith. We act upon what we believe is true. At the time of Christopher Columbus, scientists believed that the world was flat. As a result, they would not sail their ships far from land because they believed they would fall off the edge (at the horizon) if they did. Even though they did not know it, there were two continents yet to be discovered. Columbus believed that he could sail straight out from Europe and get to the East Indies faster than going around Africa and India. He sailed west and discovered North and South America and world history changed. Columbus discovered scientific truth that had not been known, and the world changed.

The same thing happens when we become convinced that truths in the Scriptures, even though they contradict conventional wisdom, are true. We get a revelation of the fact that Jesus is the *"Lamb of God, who takes away the sin of the world!"* (John 1:29). When that happens, we believe that our many sins can be forgiven and we can start a new life. This happened for me more than fifty years ago. I was quite aware of the fact that I was guilty enough to be judged by God. However, one night an evangelist shared that Jesus Christ paid for our sins and that we could be forgiven and escape judgment. I received Christ that night, along with many other people who lined the altar of our little church.

As we recognize that He is the One who has been sent by God, and we respond like Peter did when He declared that he did not want to leave Jesus, because He was the only One who could give him truth that would produce abundant life (John 6:60-71). I may not understand everything in the Bible and at times, I may not like what the Bible asks me to do, but I know it is the Word of Christ. Therefore, even if I do not understand, I believe it is true and my life will be better if I obey. This happens with every truth that becomes revelation to us.

As I come to understand the Scriptures more fully, and as more and more of it becomes part of the core of my being, my life will change. I will become more like Jesus. I will leave behind my "worldly" actions and begin to look more like a citizen of heaven, my life will change.

Revelation energizes our faith, which produces action. The story from the life of Christopher Columbus illustrates that when we become convinced that something is true, our actions change. This leads to obedience. We do not really believe something is true if we are unwilling to act upon it. The story is told of a trapeze artist getting ready to walk across Niagara Falls. He had a basket. He looked at the crowd and asked them if they believed that he could safely carry someone across Niagara Falls in the basket. The crowd enthusiastically agreed that he could. Then the trapeze artist looked at a man in the crowd and said, "Sir, get in the basket!" The next action of the man in the crowd would show whether he really believed that the man could carry someone across Niagara Falls.

When we are convinced that the Word of God is true and that Jesus is the promise-keeping God He says He is, we will "get in the basket." We read that God asks us, as believers, to give 10 percent of our income to advance His Kingdom (Malachi 3:7-10). We may think, *How can I do that?* Then we say, but God asked me to do this and He is my Provider. Therefore, we obey Him in this area of giving, and see Him take care of our needs.

During the 1980s, I served on the staff of a church in Lancaster, Pennsylvania. I was in charge of the visitation team that visited those who had visited the church. On one occasion, three of us visited a young family that had just begun attending the church. During the course of the visit, we shared how Jesus could forgive their sins and change their lives. Sometime during that next week, both the husband and wife received Jesus into their lives and were born again. They did not tell anyone at the church what had happened until they came to church. They walked in and handed an envelope to one of the elders. The elder asked what was in the envelope. The husband said, "This is our tithe check. We received Jesus and we want to do this right." Later that month, the man shared how he and his wife had begun to tithe. He said, "We now have more money at the end of the month than before!" When we become convinced of the truths of God's Word, we will obey them with the assistance of the Holy Spirit.

Obedience brings great blessing. The Gospel of John, alone, shares a number of blessings that come to those who obey. Let's look at a few of them.

Freedom (John 8:31-32). Jesus tells us that the obedient keep His Word. He tells us that when we obey, we are truly His disciples. As we obey, we come to a greater understanding of what the Word means and we will gain freedom. The first blessing that obedience brings is greater revelation. It is one thing to get a mental revelation from God that we should tithe our income and that He will meet our needs, and quite another thing to have more money left at the end of the month. This may be why the young man mentioned above left his job a short time later and to attend seminary. He knew that God was calling him, but he also knew that God would provide for his needs as he left his job to go to school. Second, the passage tells us that the truth we gain will set us free. We are set free to become all that God wants us to be. We are truly free when we become the person God created us to be.

The guidance and companionship of the Holy Spirit (John 14:15-16). This Scripture tells us that the obedient receive another Comforter, the Holy Spirit. He stands alongside us and guides us like Jesus guided the disciples while He was on earth. We will not talk much about this now because Chapter 12 is dedicated to this subject.

Intimacy with God (John 14:21,23). In these verses, Jesus tells us that the Father and the Son will make themselves known to the obedient. This means two things. First, we will be involved in a process of learning more about Him and seeing our faith grow. We have seen a glimpse of God and His truth, and we have obeyed by faith. Because of this, God reveals more of Himself to us, which causes our faith to grow more. As our faith grows more, we obey more and continue to grow because we get to know Him more fully as we continue to obey. Second, and more importantly, we develop a growing personal relationship with God.

Answers to prayer (John 15:7-8). This passage tells us that when we allow Jesus to remove hindrances and fill our mind with His Word, we will be able to petition the Father, in Jesus' name, and receive the answer to our prayers. What an amazing blessing! We will spend all of Chapter 11 talking about prayer.

Joy (John 15:9-11). Jesus says that the obedient will have His joy in them. This is the joy that Jesus experienced even when He was facing the cross. We too can have joy in the middle of great difficulty by knowing God is in control. The joy mentioned here represents Jesus' character (Galatians 5:22-23). Those who are obedient become like Jesus.

Set apart for God's purposes (John 17:17). In the last prayer that Jesus prayed, prior to the crucifixion, Jesus asked the Father to *"Sanctify them by the truth...."* The word sanctify means approximately the same thing as the Old Testament word consecrate. It talks about someone or something being set aside exclusively for the purposes of God. For us as humans, this involves two different but necessary steps.

First, Jesus asks the Father to set believers apart from the world. The world is that system of religions and philosophies generated by humans, apart from the input of God and with the help of Satan, who desires to destroy our lives (John 10:10). As we have seen already, a revelation of the Word of God exposes the lies that we have believed to be true so we forsake them for genuine truth. As we come to a greater understanding of truth, we will no longer want the things that the world has to offer. We will see them as temporary at best, and destructive at worst. We will see that these things do not bring glory to God.

Second, sanctification involves being fully dedicated to God. As we become immersed in the principles of the Word of God, our thinking changes, and we are less likely to be drawn into the things of the world. Instead we reject the world, and give our lives to Jesus and His purposes. The word of God acts like a wall of protection around our minds, and thus around our lives, protecting us from the harmful and deceptive effects of the world, enabling us to bring glory to God.

ABSORBING THE WORD OF GOD

How do we get the Word of God into our lives? We have already discussed how to spend time alone with the Lord, in Chapter 7. However, we will go into more detail, in this chapter about ways we can get into the Word of God. As we recall, it is clear that just getting the Word of God into our minds is not sufficient to bring a change to our lives. Therefore, whenever we are going to encounter the Word of God, we need to pray and ask God to speak to us, so we will believe what He says with the kind of conviction that will energize our faith and change our lives. The Scriptures show us a number of ways that men and women of God have absorbed the Word of God into their lives.

Hearing the Word of God. The beginning of Church history is recorded in Acts 2, when the Holy Spirit fell on the disciples. On that day, Peter preached a powerful message and 3,000 received Jesus. The apostles now had the task of helping the new converts become obedient disciples of the Lord Jesus Christ. The answer was to meet in homes, and the apostles came and taught them what Jesus had taught them. Many things happened in those meetings, but the first thing Luke (the author of Acts) tells us is that *"They devoted themselves to the apostles teaching..."* (Acts 2:42). As a first priority, we see the apostles teaching. We see this precedent followed in our day as pastors teach their people each week. We have also developed Sunday schools, small groups, and Bible colleges to give those gifted in teaching the opportunity to teach the principles of the Word of God. I believe it is important to avail ourselves of these kinds of opportunities.

For many reasons that we will discuss later, it is crucial that believers connect with a local congregation so we can hear the preaching and teaching of the Word of God from a man or woman of God. Let me say that it is great to get teaching from TV preachers. They can add much to your knowledge and Christian experience. However, these TV preachers cannot hold you accountable, and that is an important part of our journey as we seek to follow the Lord.

Second, we find that these early disciples did not listen passively. We are told that they *devoted* themselves to the teaching. The word devoted means "to stick to like glue." These disciples listened with a heart to obey what they heard, because they knew that it was the truth of God. Therefore, listen to the Word of God every chance you get, and listen with a passion that wants to understand and obey with the Holy Spirit's help.

Reading the Word of God. God used Moses to give the Law to Israel. Based on some of the comments we have made about the Old Testament believers' failure to fulfill the will of God, we could get the idea that the Law is not good. Let's be clear on one thing. The Law is good. It was just that those who received the Law did not have the power to obey. It was the Word of God for them, and it is still part of our Scriptures. As part of the instruction that Moses gave, He told them that when they had a future king, he was to have a copy of the Law and *"he is to read it all the days of his life so that he may learn to revere the Lord his God and follow carefully all the words of this law..."* (Deuteronomy 17:19). In order to carry out his duties properly, the king was to be someone who read the Word of God daily.

You and I also have responsibilities in Kingdom work. Therefore, we too should read the Bible on a daily basis. If the truths of the Bible are the words of eternal life, we will want to learn all that we can. If you have never read the Bible, I suggest that you start with the Gospel of John. John tells us much about Jesus and how to be *fully alive*. Eventually you will want to read the entire Bible, because it is the Word of God. I would encourage you to get to the point where you read the entire Bible every year.

There may be times when God will lead you differently, but most years I suggest going through the entire Bible. If you are just getting started, you may want to bite off smaller portions, but move toward that goal. As you read, ask God to speak to you. You may then want to spend some time meditating on, or doing deeper study of passages that God highlights to you. If you read daily, it will become a wonderful habit in your life. My father-in-law, Douglas Shields, made reading the Bible in a year his goal for the last decades of his life. When his eyesight began to fade, he got a magnifying glass and read with it. In his last days, at the age of 90, when he could not read any longer, one of his favorite times of the day was when we read the Scriptures to him.

Study the Word. Study involves going deeper into the Word of God. Perhaps God has spoken to you about a subject and you desire to look into it more deeply. I suggest you use a study Bible. It will have cross references at the bottom, in the center, or in the margin that show you the verse number that is referenced, and give some other verses on the same topic. You can use a concordance, which lists Bible words and references where the word you are studying appears in the Bible. If you are interested in a topic, you can look up some or all of the verses that contain that word.[3] You may also want to consult commentaries. There are many study tools on the Internet as well.[4] One way many people study the Bible is to join a Bible study or small group that studies and discusses the Bible. Of course, if you feel led, you can attend a school of ministry, Bible college, or seminary. These are particularly helpful for those who desire to teach the Word of God as a career. Paul told Timothy *"Study to* [show] *thyself approved unto God... rightly dividing the word of truth"* (2 Timothy 2:15 KJV).

Memorize the Word. David said, *"I have hidden your word in my heart that I might not sin against you"* (Psalm 119:11). In order to be more obedient, David memorized the Word of God so that it was on the tip of his tongue to guide him. One advantage of memorizing the Word of God is that you can ponder the verse throughout the day, even when you can't open your Bible. It certainly can be a help to you as you are ministering to someone. If you have memorized a verse about the subject you are discussing, it will be fresh on your tongue for you to share. It can be particularly helpful to memorize verses that are foundational verses of the faith, or verses that show God's perspective on those areas where you had informational strongholds.

Meditate on the Word. To meditate means to ponder a verse to see all the implications of it or how it applies to your life. Let's consider Psalm 119:11, for example. Ask, "How does this verse apply to my life?" The context shows David asking how a young man can stay pure. The answer is to hide God's Word in your heart. So how does it apply? Are you having problems with your thought life? Perhaps memorizing Scripture would be helpful.

As you study you may want to ask: who said it, to whom was it written, and why? You will develop your own questions as you learn to meditate. Meditate upon the Word no matter how you take it in, whether hearing, reading, studying, or memorizing. The Word of God only benefits us if we apply it specifically to our lives.

In Summary

As God cleanses us of sin, we want to fill our lives with His Word. We get the Word of God into our lives through disciplines such as hearing, reading, studying, memorizing, and meditating on Bible verses and passages. As we engage in these disciplines, let us ask the Holy Spirit to confirm its truth in our lives (revelation). As we become convinced of these truths, our faith will be energized and we will obey the Word with the Holy Spirit's power, opening to us every blessing of God so we can live in the fullness of life.

One of the things His Word will open up to us is a powerful, effective prayer life. We will look at the prayer life of a believer in the next chapter.

ENDNOTES

1. From foundationsforfreedom.net/Topics/Bible/Bible_Canonization.html; accessed 1/23/2014.

   "Canonization describes the process by which the community of God's people accept certain scriptures as divinely inspired and authoritative. Note three special aspects of this process:

   - Progressive collection of authoritative scriptures.

   - Written by recognized anointed men of God such as prophets and apostles.

   - Recognized and accepted as authoritative by the community of God's people.

We need to remind ourselves that no one person or council made a book 'scripture.' God's church through a process over time came to a common recognition which books were indeed inspired."

2. See also Romans 12:1-3.

3. An exhaustive concordance lists every word in the Bible. Others have selected verses with the word.

4. One great tool is e-sword.net. This resource is free for the basic package. You can buy other commentaries and versions of the Bible, if you like.

CHAPTER ELEVEN

Prayer that Changes the World

Jesus came to change the world! As we discussed earlier, Jesus' earthly ministry involved recruiting and training a group of men who would commit themselves fully to Him and His plan. These leaders had been commissioned to do the same with a group of like-minded men and women who would train others. Their goal was to develop a core of disciples who would advance the Kingdom of God throughout the earth, until the end of time.

Beginning with Chapter 7, we have discussed ways that we can live life at its fullest and be effective in expanding Christ's Kingdom. Jesus said, *"If you remain in me and my words remain in you, ask whatever you wish, and it will be done for you"* (John 15:7). This Scripture tells us that when we allow God to remove hindrances from our lives (Chapter 9) and allow His Word to live in us (Chapter 10), we are ready to pray prayers that will change us—and change the world.

This is an amazing promise—every prayer answered. Perhaps the most amazing thing about this promise is that Jesus made it six times in one night (John 14:13-14, 15:7, 16:23-24,26). We will look at these verses later in the chapter.

THE PRAYER LIFE OF JESUS

We will begin our discussion by talking about the prayer life of Jesus. John records three of Jesus' prayers. Two are small, but the third takes up an entire chapter. Let's take a look at them.

John 6:11. In this passage, we find Jesus blessing a small lunch donated by a little boy. After blessing the lunch, Jesus told the disciples to distribute the food, which fed 5,000 men. Blessing is a form of prayer.

John 11:41-42. Lazarus, the friend of Jesus had died. It appeared that Jesus had come to his grave to grieve with Lazarus' sisters. However, He had something miraculous in mind. As He prepared to call Lazarus from the grave, Jesus prayed loud enough for those around Him to hear. After He prayed, He called Lazarus, asking him to come out of the grave. In His prayer, Jesus declared that the Father always heard Him. This sounds like John 15:7 where Jesus tells His hearers that He will give us whatever we ask for in prayer. Jesus had great confidence that God would answer, and we can have the same confidence.

John 17:1-26. (Please read this passage prior to reading this section.) This prayer has been called by many "Jesus' High Priestly Prayer" because His primary focus in the prayer is the Church.[1] We will outline the prayer to discover what Jesus determined was important enough to pray in His last prayer before His crucifixion.

John 17:1-5. As Jesus began His prayer, He prayed for personal concerns:

- He thanked the Father for what He (the Father) had done, during His (Jesus') years on earth.

- He asked the Father to give Him the glory He possessed, prior to His coming to earth.

John 17:6-19. Jesus then prayed for His disciples. He made it very clear that He was praying only for those who would both hear and receive His Word (John 17:6-9). In other words, He was praying for the people He could entrust Himself to (John 2:23-25). He called these committed believers "the ones the Father gave to Him." Something ought to catch our eye here. Jesus did not pray for everyone who considered themselves to be disciples, but for those who actually gave their lives to Him.

Here is what Jesus prayed for them:

- Jesus prayed that God would protect them, in His name, because He would no longer be here to protect them (John 17:11-12).

- Jesus then prayed that they would have the full measure of His joy (John 17:13). When difficulty comes, it is easy to lose the joy of our salvation. Lack of joy can negatively impact our relationship with God and hinder us from fulfilling God's purpose for our lives. Jesus asked the Father to enable His followers to walk in the fullness of His joy, even under the most difficult circumstances.

- Jesus prayed that the Father would protect them from the evil one because the world would hate them (John 17:14-15). This seemed like two different topics. However, they are quite interrelated. When man determined that he would discover right and wrong without God's assistance, he opened the door to be influenced by Satan. The enemy has assisted in developing the world system that hates Christians. The world hates Christians because they proclaim the truth of God, as found in Scripture, and do not acknowledge the thoughts and philosophies the world sees as truth.

In our own day, we have some who seek to police "**P**olitical **C**orrectness." Many who seek to interpret and police what PC means have gone way beyond seeking justice and have determined that almost any lifestyle is acceptable. They do not include Christianity, because it declares that not every lifestyle is beneficial, and communicates that those who sin miss the mark and fail to live the abundant life God has planned for humankind. Therefore, the PC police seek to eliminate every vestige of Christianity, such as seeking to remove crosses from the workplace, even when worn as jewelry, or removing manger scenes from government property. They do this to quiet voices they perceive to be intolerant, even though Christianity represents humanity's only hope for being *fully alive.*

The world system, influenced by the devil, has always opposed God. The psalmist says, *"Why do the nations conspire and the peoples plot in vain? The kings of the earth rise up and the rulers band together against the Lord and against his anointed, saying, "Let us break their chains and throw off their shackles"* (Psalm 2:1-3). Satan has always opposed God's plan. He has sought to throw off everything that seems to restrict behavior, because he knows that when people have "freedom" to engage in every type of behavior, they will be in bondage and under his control.

As the world presses in on Christians, we can become discouraged because of this worldly pressure motivated by hatred. Therefore, Jesus wants believers to experience His joy, so they can continue to proclaim truth under difficult circumstances.

- Jesus prays that God would sanctify them in truth (John 17:17-19). We discussed this in detail in the last chapter.

John 17:20-26. Jesus told us that He was not just praying for His earthly disciples, but all those who would come to the Lord through their ministry. He said that the prayers He prayed for His earthly disciples were being prayed for true disciples in every age. He prayed, *"that all of them may be one, Father, just as you are in me and I am in you. May they also be in us so that the world may believe that you have sent me. I have given them the glory that you gave me, that they may be one as we are one—I in them and you in me—so that they may be brought to complete unity. Then the world will know that you sent me and have loved them even as you have loved me"* (John 17:21-23).

I find it interesting that Jesus says that He gave His glory to them so that they can walk in unity. We often seek after His glory so we can see the power of God work in and through us to work miracles. This is valid. However, Jesus said that His glory makes it possible for believers to walk in unity. We may ask why Jesus so desperately wants the Church to walk in unity. First, He wants us to demonstrate love. We did things because of what we would get out of them. When He changes us, we will love and walk in unity with other believers—believers who do not agree with us on every theological point, believers who don't like the same kind of worship music we do, and believers who come from diverse ethnic and socio-economic backgrounds. As we get along, the world gets a demonstration of God's power to change us.

Second, He prays for unity in the Body of Christ because this love is a powerful evangelistic tool. Note that He says that if the Body of Christ walks in unity, the world will believe that the Father sent Jesus. This is a key in seeing people come to Christ in our day because one-fifth of the world's population believes that Mohammad was the prophet sent by Allah (Arabic word for God). In addition, nearly that many people believe in one of the 330 million gods of Hinduism, and others worship inanimate objects. In the West, we worship humankind's ability to solve the world's problems through science and politics. If the world recognized that the One sent by the Father is Jesus, they would embrace Him as Lord and Savior! They would seek to live by His eternal words! The world would be a different place!

Jesus said that if we walk in unity, the world would recognize that God had sent Him. Then He indicates that if we walk in unity, the world will know that the Father loves us as much as He loves Jesus. Imagine the world knowing that the Father loves them as much as the Sent One. What would happen if the world would recognize that the Father loves them, that He is not seeking to restrict their lives, but rather to make their lives *fully alive*?

During World War II, men from many ethnic and socio-economic groups and nations fought side by side to defeat the totalitarian goals of Hitler. Jesus declared that if the worldwide Body of Christ lived like that, they would advance the Kingdom of God with great effectiveness.

As Jesus ended His prayer, He declared that He would continue to make the Father known to them. This means that He would continue to give His disciples new revelation of His greatness, which would energize their faith and motivate them to greater obedience. This obedience would enable them to live life at its fullest.

The Focus of Jesus' Prayers

I find it interesting that Jesus' prayers focused solely upon issues that would enable His people to advance His Kingdom. Jesus was facing a horrible death. He could have focused His prayer on Himself and His present difficulty. He did not do that. Instead, He prayed that His committed disciples would change the world. Shouldn't our prayers follow His example?

About this time you may wonder, *Do you mean I can't pray for personal things?* Of course you can. Paul told the church in Philippi that they should not be nervous about anything, but pray about everything (Philippians 4:4-6). In Jesus' model prayer, He instructed His disciples to pray about their daily bread (Matthew 6:11).

We need to pray about the things that concern our lives. However, should these concerns form the bulk of our prayers? At one point, Jesus talked about people who worried about their food and clothing. He told them, *"But seek first his kingdom and his righteousness, and all these things will be given to you as well"* (Matthew 6:33). In saying this, Jesus made it clear that if you make the Kingdom of God your number one priority, God will take care of your day-to-day needs. Paul told the Philippians, *"And my God will meet all your needs according to the riches of his glory in Christ Jesus"* (Philippians 4:19). If we follow God, He will take care of us.

If we are honest, we must admit that many of our prayers revolve around our needs, the needs God has promised to meet. In the United States, we often pray about "American Dream" stuff. Does this reveal that we are more committed to our security and comfort than advancing the Kingdom?

A brief look at the prayers recorded in the other Gospels will confirm that Jesus prayed for Kingdom issues and implies that we should do the same.

- *Matthew 4:1-11.* As Jesus reached adulthood, He prepared for His official earthly ministry. Matthew tells us that He spent forty days in fasting-prayer. The result was that the Holy Spirit came upon Him and He ministered in power for the next three and one half years.

- *Luke 6:12-16.* In order for the ministry to go forward after He went back to heaven, Jesus needed to train key men who would carry on after He was gone. However, who should He choose to train to continue His ministry after He left? Jesus spent an entire night in prayer asking God to reveal whom He should choose.

- Matthew 6:9-13. It was mentioned earlier that the Lord's Prayer is a model prayer that Jesus gave to the disciples when they wanted to learn how to pray. Nearly the entire prayer focuses upon Kingdom issues. Even the prayer for daily bread focuses on the Kingdom, because we need our sustenance in order to fulfill the will of God.

Although the Gospel writers did not record every prayer of Jesus, we can safely assume that the Holy Spirit inspired the Gospel writers to record the prayers that would be most instructive to His followers. Therefore, if we are to be like Jesus, much of our prayer life will focus on the advancement of God's Kingdom.

Jesus' Amazing Promise

At the beginning of this chapter you read that Jesus made the promise six times in one night that we could ask for anything we wished, and He would do it. Although these promises seem to be nearly identical, they appear in different contexts. Let's look at Jesus' promise in each context to learn how Jesus wants us to pray.

Believe me when I say that I am in the Father and the Father is in me; or at least believe on the evidence of the works themselves. Very truly I tell you, whoever believes in me will do the works I have been doing, and they will do even greater things than these, because I am going to the Father. And I will do whatever you ask in my name, so that the Father may be glorified in the

Son. You may ask me for anything in my name, and I will do it (John 14:11-14).

Jesus made a number of mind-boggling promises in this passage. First, He told His disciples that they would do what He had been doing. I believe we all agree that this involves everything that He did during His earthly ministry, but there is an emphasis on the works, the miracles. If Jesus needed miracles to demonstrate that He had been sent by God, His followers would need the same kind of authentication to inspire people to listen to them. We should trust the Father to perform miracles in our lives, so we gain a hearing among those who need Him.

During our trip to India in September 2013, a man had agreed to cook for a group of pastors and wives for an evening meeting. However, he was quite sick with a kidney condition. A group of believers prayed for him. He immediately said that he felt 75 percent better. When he arrived to cook, he said he was completely well! The Father had done a work through faith-filled prayer. This brought glory to God and provided a testimony for those who knew what God had done.

Jesus also told His disciples that they would do greater works than He had done. How could Jesus' followers do greater works than Him? He explained during a discussion with some who opposed Him for healing a man on the Sabbath. Jesus told His accusers that He would do greater works than the healing of the lame man. He explained what He meant by "greater works" by explaining that the Father gave Him the responsibility to choose who would receive the life God offered. He declared that those who believe in Him would receive this life (John 5:16-24). The greater work is seeing people pass from death to life. It is seeing people born again, who see and enter the Kingdom of God. The Church that has followed Jesus has seen millions, perhaps billions come to Christ, in the past 2,000 years. They have done the greater work on a larger scale than He did. This promise tells us that

Jesus will use us to perform miracles that will pave the way to preach the Gospel.

In Jesus' Name. Because Jesus promised that we would do the things that He did, and the greater work of seeing people come to and grow in Jesus, we must conclude that we will only receive these things as we pray. He further tells His readers that the kind of prayer that receives these amazing answers is prayer in Jesus' name. What does it mean to pray in Jesus name? We have become so accustomed to adding these words at the end of every prayer that we may have lost Jesus' meaning. If you close your prayers this way, it is perfectly okay, especially if you allow the words to remind you what Jesus meant when He told us to pray in His name.

To pray "in Jesus' name" is to ask for the things that He would ask for. This might disappoint some, because they're looking for a formula that guarantees they will receive everything they want. The truth is, all the things we want may not be beneficial to us personally, and might not assist in advancing the Kingdom. Some of them may actually harm us. However, the people who have immersed their minds in God's eternal Word will begin to gain God's perspective on life. When God's people have His perspective, they will ask for those things that are truly beneficial, the things that Jesus would ask for.

If you remain in me and my words remain in you, ask whatever you wish, and it will be done for you (John 15:7).

This verse talks about walking in the kind of intimacy with God that enables Him to remove hindrances from our lives, and impart wisdom through His eternal Word. We have already talked about this promise in great detail in Chapters 9 and 10. In this verse, John records Jesus' promise to answer prayer in the context of bearing spiritual fruit. As we have discussed previously, this fruit occurs as our character becomes more like Jesus and as we grow in our effectiveness in ministry.

We find that the key to bearing fruit is prayer, energized because we remain in Him and His Word remains in us. When we remain in Him and His Word remains in us, we know what He desires. When we understand what He wants, we will go to Him in prayer and ask Him to do it. Jesus answers these prayers. They are prayers *"in Jesus name."* James tells us *"The prayer of a righteous person is powerful and effective"* (James 5:16). We may ask why we need to pray for the things that God already wants to do. There are a couple of reasons. God wants us to come to that point in our lives where we only want what He wants and we trust Him to meet our needs. When we reach that point, God can entrust Himself to us. When He trusts us like that, He gives us world-changing answers to prayers and assignments.

> *In that day you will no longer ask me anything. Very truly I tell you, my Father will give you whatever you ask in my name. Until now you have not asked for anything in my name. Ask and you will receive, and your joy will be complete. ...In that day you will ask in my name. I am not saying that I will ask the Father on your behalf* (John 16:23-26).

Jesus acknowledges that His disciples would experience grief when He went back to heaven, but that much good would come from His departure. He promised them that they would have a joy that would not be taken away from them. This kind of joy comes from knowing that there is always *Someone* who will listen to us. Because Jesus has gone, we, His followers, can go into the presence of the Father in heaven who is available at any time and for any reason.

- We can talk to Him about anything. Remember Philippians 4:4-6. Sometimes it is cathartic to know that He listens. When I was in seminary, the church that I served hired a new pastor. They wanted to make it possible for him to hire his own staff so they let me go. This was painful. The next day I talked to a good friend at the seminary. He had had the same experience. As I looked into his eyes and knew that he understood, I experienced a level of healing.[2] Sometimes it helps just to talk to the Father. He understands!

- We can talk to Him about those places where we are not yet like Jesus. He will help us.

- We can talk with Him about the issues that assist in advancing His Kingdom around the world: What is my role? What do You want to do in the lives of those to whom I minister? When we get answers to these questions, we can ask Him to make it happen. In addition to this, we can ask Him what is on His heart for our city and world. When we pray in His name, good things happen. Hallelujah!

PRAYERS AND PRAYING

So how do we get involved in prayer? The following suggestions are guidelines for you to adopt and adapt to your particular lifestyle and ministry.

1. As we get started, let's remember that prayer is talking with God. We don't have to recite certain religious words or phrases to be effective. When a baby is small, he cannot say many words, but mom and dad don't care about the correctness of those first few words. They are just so happy to hear the child speak to them. So get started! Don't worry if you are saying it right. God is happy that you want to talk with Him and He knows how to interpret your heart.

2. Pray about everything (Philippians 4:4-6).

3. Look to the Scriptures to determine what God wants us to pray about.

a. The Lord's Prayer. In the Lord's Prayer, we find the following topics:

- Acknowledge and bask in the fact that He is our Father.

- Worship. His name is holy. As we get to know Him, we will tell Him how awesome He is as we pray.

- Pray for God's Kingdom to come in our lives, in the people that we know, and for the peoples of the world.

- Pray for your daily bread. This includes our food and also the things that we need daily to live and serve the Lord. It can be shelter, transportation, money, or people to help us minister; what you need to fulfill God's purpose in your life.

- As part of our prayer lives, we are asked to forgive others. If not, our prayers will be hindered.

- We are to pray that we do not fall into temptation, and that we do not come under the control of the evil one.

b. Read the Psalms. Many of them are prayers.

c. As you read Paul's letters, look at his prayers (Philippians 1:9-11; Colossians 1:9-13; and others).

4. Set time aside to be with the Lord. If we set a specific time each day, we are more likely to pray consistently. Of course we will want to pray throughout the day, but it is good to set a time aside to make sure that we pray on a

regular basis. My wife and I walk and pray almost every morning. It is generally the first thing we do after we have each spent time personally with the Lord.

5. Pray with others.

   a. You will learn effective ways to pray, as you pray with others.

   b. Read Matthew 18:19-20. In this passage Jesus tells us that when we pray together there is greater effectiveness than when we pray alone. We can pray together in the same location, or we can agree to pray about the same topics even when apart. Our friend in Pakistan gives specific prayer points to believers throughout the nation. They cannot be together every time they pray, but they can pray about the same requests.

6. Keep a prayer journal.

   a. Keep a record of your prayer requests, and then write down how God answers them.

   b. You may want to write out your prayers.

   c. Write down what God says to you from His Word.

Don't feel guilty if you don't engage in all of these. They are merely suggestions that can assist you in your prayer life. Use those that help you most.

IN SUMMARY

Prayer can change the world. I challenge you again to let Jesus get rid of the hindrances in your life and fill your mind with His Word. As you do this, you will learn what He desires. As you come to a greater understanding of what He wants, pray for those things. You will be praying "in His name" and changing the world!

ENDNOTES

1. There are some who reason that this prayer should actually be called the Lord's Prayer, because it is the prayer that Jesus prayed, and what we call the Lord's Prayer is actually a teaching tool designed by Jesus to teach His disciples what our prayers should focus upon.

2. There was much more to come, but this was the beginning.

CHAPTER TWELVE

Empowered
by the Holy Spirit

We had just completed a training seminar in the State of Gujarat in India, and had begun to travel to our next seminar city in the State of Maharashtra. Not long after entering Maharashtra, the driver asked us to look for a gas station. We looked and looked, but we did not see any. Eventually we wound up sitting alongside the road in a fully functioning SUV, yet with no "petrol" to power the vehicle.

It has been noted that many Old Testament saints failed to fulfill the will of God because they did not possess the power to live as God intended. The Holy Spirit supplies all of the grace we need to live life as He desires. John frequently talks about the Holy Spirit because his Gospel focuses on how we can live life to the fullest. In fact, he refers to the Holy Spirit, calling Him: Holy Spirit, Spirit, Counselor, and Living Water, twenty-seven times in the twenty-one chapters in his Gospel.

In this chapter we will discover how the Holy Spirit enables us to be fully alive and how we can access this power for living.

JESUS' HOLY SPIRIT-EMPOWERED LIFE

The Holy Spirit empowered Jesus' earthly life (John 1:29-34). John the Baptist knew that he had been sent to prepare the way for the Prophet-King. On one occasion, as he walked along the road with his disciples, John saw Jesus and declared that He is the Lamb of God that will take away the world's sins. John knew that Jesus was the One sent by God, because God had told him that He would reveal the One by having the Holy Spirit descend upon Him, like a dove. When John the Baptist saw the Holy Spirit descend on Jesus, he knew that He was the One. We find three other important truths about the Holy Spirit in this passage in John 1.

1. *The Spirit remained on Jesus.* During Old Testament times, the Holy Spirit rested upon people for short periods of time, to enable them to fulfill a specific task, such as King Saul prophesying to establish that God intended to use him as king (1 Samuel 10:5-7). However, He did not remain on them, as He does for believers today.

2. *Jesus lived by the power of the Holy Spirit during His time on earth.* John the Baptist tells us, for example, that Jesus spoke the Word of God by the Spirit (John 3:34).

3. *John the Baptist said that the One upon whom the Spirit rested would also baptize others in the Holy Spirit.* Not only was the Holy Spirit the Source of Jesus' power, but He is the Source of power for every believer through the ages. Paul told the believers at Rome *"...And if anyone does not have the Spirit of Christ, they do not belong to Christ"* (Romans 8:9). When we receive Jesus Christ, we are born again because the Holy Spirit, the Spirit of

Christ, comes to live in us. The Holy Spirit is every believer's Source of life (John 3:3-8).

Later, John talks about the Holy Spirit as he recounts a discussion between Jesus and Nicodemus. Jesus told Nicodemus that someone can only see the Kingdom of God if the person is born again. He goes on to explain that someone is born again when the Holy Spirit enters the person and produces spiritual life.

Men and women must be born again by the Spirit, because when Adam and Eve sinned, the Spirit of God left them. They died spiritually. However, whenever people repent of their sins and ask Jesus to give them a new life, the Holy Spirit enters their human spirit and brings them to life spiritually. Jesus said that this new life is not something we can see, but we can see the results, just like we see the results of wind, even though we don't see it (John 3:8).

My wife and I had some wonderful friends who ministered to a young man who had become addicted to prescription drugs, prescribed because of emotional problems. Our friends showed the love of Jesus to the young man for months, and finally suggested that he come to see me. He was ready to give his life to Jesus. After he came to Christ, he began to work with his doctor to get off the drugs. He was finally able to stop taking these drugs. When this began, he would tell me how many days he had been off the pills, with no emotional difficulty. One day, he could not remember how many days it had been. I knew that this was a turning point. Before coming to Christ, he could not live without the drugs. As the Spirit of God began to change him, he no longer needed them. We could not physically see the Spirit of God working in his life, but we saw His impact.

Jesus told a Samaritan woman *"the water I give them will become in them a spring of water welling up to eternal life"* (John 4:14, see also John 7:37-39). The water represents the life produced by the Holy

Spirit. He says that this life wells up in such a way that eternal life, the life of Jesus, is produced in those who receive Him.

When the Holy Spirit comes into our lives, we are born again. We are truly alive—spirit, soul, and body—for the very first time.

Worship By the Power of the Holy Spirit

Jesus rested near a well while His disciples went into a nearby village to get some food. While Jesus rested there, He talked to the Samaritan woman mentioned in John 4. As they talked, Jesus turned the discussion to spiritual things. During the discussion, the woman said that the Jews and Samaritans worship on different mountains, and she asked Him to tell her who was right. Finally, Jesus said, *"Yet a time is coming and has now come when the true worshipers will worship the Father in the Spirit and in truth, for they are the kind of worshipers the Father seeks"* (John 4:23).

Jesus was saying, "We have moved into a new era when we do not need to find the right location to worship, but rather worship springs from within, guided by truth and empowered by the Holy Spirit." We might ask, "Does this mean we don't need to go to church to worship?" The answer to this question is yes and no. It is good to meet together to declare the wonders of God. As we will see in the next chapter, God tells us that Christians need to meet together to be as effective as possible. This fellowship with other believers is for encouragement and instruction, but also to declare the greatness of God through testimony and song.

However, we do not need to be in the church to worship. In fact, Paul tells the Corinthians three times that believers are the temple of God. (See First Corinthians 3:16, 6:19 and Second Corinthians 6:16.) We are the place of worship. Although we can worship on our own, we also need to worship with others as well. I knew a man who told me that he wanted to follow Jesus. Then he asked me, "Can I do this Christian thing alone?" (He preferred being alone.) I said, "No." It is important to worship together in our churches or homes, but we must also recognize that we are God's temple. We can worship anywhere.

Most of us understand worship as what we do in church. In fact, for many it is what we do before the sermon, which often includes the reading of Scriptures, declaring the greatness of God, the giving of testimonies of God's work in the lives of individuals and the singing of songs that express our love and devotion to Him. *This is worship!* However, there is much more to worship.

The Book of Romans lays out the blessings of our salvation. Paul spends the first eight chapters talking about all that Jesus has provided through His death and resurrection. Paul then takes a break and discusses God's work among the Jewish people. At the end of Romans 11, Paul is so overwhelmed by the greatness of God's plan that he breaks out in song (Romans 11:33-36). Immediately after his personal worship service, Paul tells his readers how to live in light of what God has done for them. He says, *"Therefore, I urge you, brothers and sisters, in view of God's mercy, to offer your bodies as a living sacrifice, holy and pleasing to God—this is your true and proper worship"* (Romans 12:1). Paul says that worship is not just singing words, but rather it is the giving of our lives to Him.

After all, we can't truly say that He is Lord, if we do not do what He says. We can't say that we believe He knows what is best for us, if we maintain veto power. We can't truly talk about how much He loves us and wants what is best for us, if we do not do what His love asks us to do. Our obedience is worship! As we learned in Chapter 10, our obedience produces joy (John 15:11) and a relationship with the Father, Son, and Holy Spirit (John 14:15,21,23). When we obey Him, we begin to experience fullness of life. As we experience His goodness through obedience, we will want to verbally declare His wonder and goodness, which is what we normally think of as worship. We do all of this by the power of the Holy Spirit.

THE HOLY SPIRIT'S TEACHINGS AND REVELATIONS

The Holy Spirit teaches us the Word of God in such a way that we receive revelation, which produces life in us.

We have seen throughout this book that John puts a great deal of emphasis on the Word of God. He also emphasizes the Holy Spirit's role in placing the Word of God in our lives. In Chapter 10, we established the fact that the Holy Spirit inspired the Bible's human writers to write down the very words of God. It is difficult to detect a difference in the roles of the Holy Spirit and the Word of God when it comes to enabling us to live as God desires us to live. This is seen when we look at two sets of parallel passages[2] from the Scriptures.

The first parallel passages are found in Colossians 3:16 and Ephesians 5:18-19. In Ephesians 5:19, Paul says, *"speaking to one another with psalms, hymns, and songs from the Spirit. Sing and make music from your heart to the Lord."* In Colossians 3:16, he says, *"as you teach and admonish one another with all wisdom through psalms, hymns and songs from the Spirit, singing to God with gratitude in your hearts."* These two passages clearly talk about the same topic, yet Colossians 3:16 tells us to *"Let the message* [Word] *of Christ dwell among you richly..."* and Ephesians 5:18 exhorts us to *"be filled with the Spirit."*

The second set of parallel verses is John 17:17-19 and John 20:21-23. In both cases, Jesus tells His disciples that He is sending them, as the Father had sent Him. In the first passage, Jesus prays for them to be sanctified in the truth, the Word of God; and in the second, Jesus breathes on them to receive the Holy Spirit. The Word of God, and the Holy Spirit work together to make us like Jesus. As we read or study, the Holy Spirit gives us revelation by highlighting passages that minister to us.

Unfortunately, some churches in the United States consider themselves to be "Word churches," while others boast of being "Spirit churches." In reality, if churches are not both, they are neither. If we love the Word of God, we must honor the One who inspired its writing and whose illumination gives us understanding of that Word, giving energy to our faith. If we pride ourselves in being "a Spirit church," we will fully love and respect Him by also seeking to understand "The Book" He wrote.

When we look at the Holy Spirit as Counselor, we understand His role better. The word *Paraclete,* which is translated Counselor, talks about someone who is a friend, and particularly a legal friend. Now we may wonder what this has to do with the Word of God. I will illustrate this with a personal experience. Recently, my mother passed away. She had been on Medicaid, and in order to make sure that we did everything legally correct in caring for her affairs, we consulted a lawyer. We could read the laws, but it took the skill of a lawyer, trained in this field, to tell us how to interpret and apply them.

Similarly, because the Holy Spirit wrote the Scriptures, He understands exactly what each passage means and He knows exactly how it applies to our lives at any given time. It is wonderful that we have the written Word of God, but we sometimes use our human reasoning to interpret the Scriptures. (See Second Peter 3:16.) We may wonder, as did Pilate, "What is truth?" The blessing for us is that we know the Author of the Word of God. He reveals truth to those who obey.

THE HOLY SPIRIT OF TRUTH

On three occasions, Jesus called the Holy Spirit, *"the Spirit of truth."* In John 14:17, Jesus told His disciples that the Spirit of truth would be in them. When He said this, Jesus told His disciples that the

Holy Spirit would live in them so He could give them direction. In John 14:26, Jesus said that He would help them remember what He had said, and teach them everything else they needed to know. Jesus undoubtedly had in mind the fact that the Holy Spirit would enable the Gospel writers to remember what He said, then they could accurately write it down and give new teaching to Peter, Paul, James, Jude, and John so they could write the remainder of the New Testament.

In addition, Jesus had something in mind for all believers seeking to obey Him. He said, *"The Spirit gives life; the flesh counts for nothing. The words I have spoken to you—they are Spirit and life"* (John 6:63). Jesus meant that the words He spoke were inspired by the Holy Spirit (see John 3:34), and they would produce life in those who responded to Him. Therefore, we conclude that the Holy Spirit will take the words written on the pages of our Bibles, and use them to change the way we think and the way we live. He takes the written Word and gives us revelation that produces life.

The third time Jesus calls the Holy Spirit "the Spirit of truth," He told His disciples that the Holy Spirit would guide them into truth. He tells us the same—the Holy Spirit not only gives information, He also gives understanding that changes our perspective, producing obedience. He guides us out of worldly living into Kingdom living.

Holy Spirit-Produced Evangelism and Missions

The last time John used the word *Paraclete* in his Gospel, he told his readers that He, the Holy Spirit, would testify of Jesus. This means two things. First, He will continue to give believers greater understanding of who Jesus is so they can be even more like Jesus. Second, He testifies to those who do not yet know Jesus. Those who receive Jesus must have the Word of God shared with them in a way that stimulates them to embrace Jesus and the life He offers. He does this in two ways. He speaks through believers who share their testimony and tells others about Jesus.

Immediately, after saying that the Spirit will testify of Him, Jesus told the believers that *they* would testify of Him (John 15:26-27). However, for the preaching³ of the Gospel to be effective, those receiving the message must receive revelation so the message they have heard is true. This revelation will stimulate them to exercise faith in Jesus and follow Him. When Paul talked about his experience in sharing the Gospel with believers in Corinth, he said, *"My message and my preaching were not with wise and persuasive words, but with a demonstration of the Spirit's power"* (1 Corinthians 2:4). The Spirit of God convinced some of the people in Corinth that what Paul said was true. They believed, and a church was formed.

We see this in the life of the early Church. The 120 received the Holy Spirit; Peter preached the Gospel, and 3,000 received Christ. As we read Acts 2, we find that Peter did not give an altar call, rather the people asked what they needed to do to be saved. In effect, they asked Peter, "We believe what you are telling us is true. Now what do we do about it?" How can we explain their response, apart from the convicting power of the Holy Spirit?

Jesus tells us that the Holy Spirit convinces people of their need to come to Christ, in three ways (John 16:8-11).

1. *The Holy Spirit will convict them of sin.* Jesus tells us that people will be convicted of sin, because they do not believe in Him. Every person has sinned. Those who have not yet received Christ remain in sin, and continue to miss out on all that life could be. He lets them know that they are sinners who can be forgiven because of Christ's death on the cross.

2. *The Holy Spirit convinces them of righteousness, because Jesus is no longer with them.* When Jesus walked on earth,

He demonstrated righteous living. As believers in Jesus, we are becoming more and more righteous, but not perfect. The Holy Spirit shows unbelievers what righteousness is to show them what life could be, and to show them how short of that life they are.

3. *The Holy Spirit convinces them that judgment has come on the prince of the world, and therefore judgment will come to them.* When Jesus rose from the grave and ascended to be with the Father, the prince of the world was defeated and judged for his rebellion. When the Holy Spirit convinces the unbeliever that Satan has been found guilty, He also shows him that he is guilty, apart from the forgiveness of Jesus. I personally came to Christ because the Holy Spirit convinced me that I deserved judgment. Because of this, I gave my life to Him.

The Holy Spirit also does supernatural deeds, which draw people to Jesus. This includes the miraculous signs, which cause some people to listen to the preaching and testimony of believers. In recent decades, we have become aware of miraculous dreams coming to Muslims. These have taken two forms. First, they see a Man in white that they know is Jesus. They are so impressed with Him, that they seek to learn more. This has happened to individuals and to groups of Muslims. In the second form of the dream, Muslims see an actual person. They are told that when they see this person, they should talk to him because the person will tell them the truth. Generally, a short time later, they see the person who had appeared in their dream, and are led to Jesus.

As believers, we need the Holy Spirit's power to witness to others. The Holy Spirit makes it possible for us to be effective in leading others to Him through the testimony of our changed lives. (More on this in Chapter 14.)

ACCESSING THE HOLY SPIRIT'S POWER

As we recognize our need for the Holy Spirit, we may ask, "How can I have His power in my life?" I want to mention four things in answer to this question:

1. *Be born again by receiving Christ as your Savior and Lord.*
   We are born again of the Spirit of God. Paul has told us that if we don't have the Spirit, we are none of His. When we receive Christ, the Holy Spirit enters our human spirit and we begin a new life. So, if you have not given your life to Christ, do so right now.

2. *Be filled with or baptized in the Holy Spirit.* We are baptized in or filled with the Spirit when He comes in power to enable us to advance the Kingdom. We get a glimpse of that power as we read the Book of Acts. We receive the Holy Spirit when we are born again. However, many people do not immediately begin to walk in His power. When believers realize they lack the Spirit's power to live for Christ and reach others for Him, they ask the Holy Spirit to come upon them in power. Some believers call this the baptism of the Spirit; others call it being filled with the Spirit. When people are filled or baptized with the Spirit, their lives and ministries have greater impact, because they are living by the power of the Holy Spirit. Often the believer's spiritual gifts begin to become more evident and effective at this time (more in Chapter 14). Those who give their lives completely to Jesus can be empowered by the Holy Spirit simply by asking. He wants to fill us.

3. *Seek the Holy Spirit's direction.*

   - Each day as you get up, ask the Holy Spirit to direct your life.

- Ask the Holy Spirit to teach and direct you as you read His Word.

- Develop the art of listening to the Holy Spirit. He will direct you. He may place an idea on your heart, or you may have a deep conviction that seems to be coming from inside (your human spirit is there). The first time my wife and I planned to travel to Pakistan, things got really bad there a few days before we left. A major magazine declared Pakistan to be the most dangerous country in the world. General Musharraf, the president of Pakistan at the time, declared marshal law. Friends began to ask if we were going. I must admit that I wondered if we should cancel. However, my wife knew from the Holy Spirit that we were to go. We went, and God did a great work and gave us great ministry connections. We have been there three more times and plan to continue going as often as the Lord allows us. As you learn to hear the voice of the Holy Spirit, it would be advisable to share what you are hearing with a mature believer. The person will give you input and help you grow in your ability to hear God.

- Obey what He says, by His power.

4. *Do not grieve the Holy Spirit (Ephesians 4:30).* Grieving the Holy Spirit is making Him sad. I believe the Holy Spirit is saddened when He comes into people's lives who continue to live like they did when they were in the world. We grieve Him by failing to commit our lives to Jesus and allowing Him to renew our minds in the Word. We grieve Him when we hear His voice, but resist obeying Him. Eventually, we will not hear His voice at all.

In Summary

As believers, the Holy Spirit lives in us. He wants us to live righteously as Kingdom citizens. The Holy Spirit makes this possible by teaching us truth, guiding our lives, and supplying power for our daily life and ministry. Ask Him to direct you and fill you so you can obey Him.

ENDNOTES

1. I personally believe this doxology was a song, but it may be a spoken word of praise. In either case, Paul could not contain himself and broke into praise.

2. When I talk of a parallel passage, I mean two passages that talk of the same topic.

3. By "preaching of the Gospel," I refer to any means we participate in that shares Christ with those who do not know Him. This might be sharing a testimony, sharing the plan of salvation with someone, engaging in compassionate ministry, or an actual sermon in a church or stadium.

CHAPTER THIRTEEN

Connect to a Like-Minded, Loving Family

Jesus sent His followers into a hostile world in order to present the love of His Father to the people who lived there. He knew that they would face rejection and persecution, but He also knew that they could fulfill His plan, if they committed themselves fully to Him and accessed the grace God had provided for them. We have already talked about several aspects of this grace: His ability to remove our character flaws and the sins that hinder us, His life-changing Word, His promise to answer prayers prayed in Jesus' name, and the indwelling power of the Holy Spirit. In this chapter, we will talk about another way God has lavished His grace upon us—He connects us to a like-minded, loving family!

Who Else Is Gonna Love Ya?

Jesus told Nicodemus that people see and enter the Kingdom of God when they are born again. You read in Chapter 1 that Adam and Eve wanted to discover what was right and wrong, but decided they would like to make their discoveries on their own, apart from God. Unfortunately, since the Fall, humankind has come up with a whole system of religions and philosophies that lead people away from truth. The Bible calls this "the world system" or simply "the world." In the context of telling the disciples to love one another (John 15:12,17), Jesus said:

If the world hates you, keep in mind that it hated me first. If you belonged to the world, it would love you as its own. As it is, you do not belong to the world, but I have chosen you out of the world. That is why the world hates you (John 15:18-19).

When we are born again, we begin to understand God's truth. As we begin to grow in this new understanding, we begin to live by Kingdom principles, and give our lives to advancing the Kingdom of God. This new God-centered life puts us at odds with the world because our priorities are now different from theirs. The world opposes committed believers because those in the world believe that the committed believers are wrong about life. The world opposes believers because their lifestyle and preaching expose the places where those in the world have sinned (fallen short of what their lives could be). They complain that believers are intolerant, wondering who or what gives them the right to determine what is right and wrong. They wonder how believers could be so narrow-minded and arrogant as to say that there is only one way to God. The world despises believers because they proclaim that immoral lifestyles do not produce the most fulfilling life.

This hatred of believers has led to persecution. It began with Jesus and the apostles, and continues into our day, in both Communist and Islamic nations, through intimidation, imprisonment, torture, and even the killing of those who refuse to recant their faith. An example is Asia Bibi, a Pakistani Christian imprisoned for breaking the Islamic government's blasphemy law, because she expressed her belief about Jesus. She has been in prison for a number of years, separated from her husband and children.

In other places, like the U.S., the rejection is less severe. But more and more in the "Christian West," we see people ridiculed because they have not accepted the interpretation of the PC police, some of whom have determined that even if our religious beliefs differ from their concept of justice, that the person or even religion must be quieted. The more radical of these "police" want us to tolerate every possible lifestyle regardless what the Scriptures teach. Some believers have been overlooked for promotions because they will not engage in activities that they believe are offensive to God. One man I know has been passed over for promotions because he won't drink alcoholic beverages, which he believed the Lord had instructed him not to drink, with clients, an activity the employer unfortunately felt necessary to gain sales.

Because Jesus knew all of this, He told His disciples to love one another. He knew His disciples would have to advance God's Kingdom under difficult circumstances, and would need the support of like-minded believers.

LIKE-MINDED BELIEVERS

Before we go any further, I want to comment on what I mean by like-minded believers. Right from the beginning of the book, it was explained that Jesus searches for believers to whom He could entrust the ministry of the Gospel when He went back to heaven. He didn't just take the first followers who came along, but rather looked for those to whom He could entrust Himself. God has always been like that. He told King Asa, *"For the eyes of the Lord range throughout the earth to strengthen those who hearts are fully committed to him"* (2 Chronicles 16:9). These fully committed people are the only ones He can strengthen, because they are the only ones who will seek, by the grace of God, to obey the Word of God.

These are the kind of believers Jesus wants us to connect with. These are the ones we can lock arms with, so that together we can take the Gospel to the ends of the earth. This is biblical fellowship. The others are only playing at Christianity.

But the Body of Christ is so diverse, how can we have this kind of fellowship? There are many differences among those who are part of the Body of Christ. We have different tastes created by the differences in our upbringing and our ethnicity. We don't interpret every aspect of the Scriptures the same. As we have traveled to different parts of the world, we have found that believers have allowed their differences to create schisms in the Body. Some find it hard to work with Christians who believe differently about certain theological hot topics. A few decades ago, the hot question among so many believers was whether they could lose their salvation. Believers felt uncomfortable fellowshipping with those who held opposing views on the subject. However, is this an important question? If every believer would just live the way God desires, it wouldn't matter whether we can lose our salvation.

At various times and in different locations, the Body of Christ deals with other questions, such as worship styles or what it means to be filled with or baptized in the Holy Spirit. Again, there are ways to resolve these questions if we are willing to listen to one another. Music touches our emotions. Different styles of music minister to different people, especially if they come from different generations; but we can accept and respect those who worship differently, knowing that their style of music is doing for them what ours does for us. We might even consider having a variety of styles of music in our worship services, so that a wider range of people might connect with God.

As far as the ministry of the Holy Spirit is concerned, I find it interesting that we argue and divide over the One God has sent to enable us to love one another. Most believers have the same fundamental beliefs about the Holy Spirit. Most I know believe we must be empowered by the Holy Spirit. Personally I see believers on both the Charismatic-Pentecostal and Evangelical sides of the Holy Spirit issue winning people to Jesus, and seeing great answers to prayer. Both demonstrate the work of the Holy Spirit in their ministries. Remember, our fellowship is with people who want to do all they can to advance the Kingdom of God. Therefore, we need to agree to disagree on nonessential issues and on doctrines where we differ yet fall within the circle of biblical orthodoxy, because disunity damages the Church's ability to advance His Kingdom on earth.

As discussed in our chapter on prayer, the unity of the Body of Christ has an impact in drawing men and women to Jesus Christ. Let's do all we can to gain and maintain unity in the Body of Christ.

LOVE ONE ANOTHER

Earlier in the same evening as this discussion, Jesus told His disciples, *"By this everyone will know that you are my disciples, if you love one another"* (John 13:35). They will know that we are His disciples because we love like He does. He was the most compassionate, caring, and loving person who ever walked the face of the earth. Our love stands as a testimony that He lives in us. After all, what other group of people really love one another? There are even schisms in Islam. During one of our trips to Pakistan, Sunni Muslims did damage to Shia Muslims during a Shia celebration. When Christians love, even when we have some differences, the world will take notice that we possess something special. *We do!*

WAYS WE CAN LEARN
TO LOVE ONE ANOTHER

Recognize that there is only one Body. We have been called the Body of Christ. We are His hands, arms, and feet on the earth. A man's body, if healthy, will do what the man wants it to do. If a man decides to go to work, his body takes him there. If he decides to push away from the table and stop eating or go for a jog, the body does what he is determined to do. This is true, unless the body of the person is diseased. Then it may rebel against him. If the Body of Christ is healthy, it will do what Christ desires, and that is to love one another and work together to advance His Kingdom throughout the earth. We all have the same purpose.

Evidently, the believers in Ephesus were struggling with the issue of unity. It seems to have been along ethnic lines. Paul said to them, *"There is one body and one Spirit, just as you were called to one hope when you were called; one Lord, one faith, one baptism; one God and Father of all, who is over all and through all and in all"* (Ephesians 4:4-6). We are one Body no matter what we may think.

We must work to maintain our unity. We must admit that it is not easy to get along with everyone, even members of the Body of Christ. There are those who believe differently from the way we do on issues that are important to us. Let me say at this point, I am not talking about people who have a different idea about how a person is saved. Jesus is the only way to God. If He had not died on the cross and rose from the dead, we would have no hope of being born again. We can only have real fellowship with those who know Christ, and who are fully committed to Him and His Kingdom.

However, as mentioned, we have brothers and sisters who differ from us on matters like how and when a person is empowered by the Holy Spirit, what style(s) of worship should we use, or what are the most effective means of evangelism? The Body of Christ, at least in the U.S., differs on political issues. Some believe in man-made global warming and others do not. Some vote Republican and some vote Democrat. Some believe in a person's right to own a gun, and others do not. We differ on what the role of government should be in the lives of people. Unfortunately, we have come to the point where we have made these issues a test of our faith.

A few years ago, I was overseeing a statewide prayer ministry. I sent an email to a woman and signed it "John, for John and Kerry." She thought that I wrote, John for John Kerry (which I did not). It was during the year when current Secretary of State, John Kerry, was running for president. The woman wrote back saying she did not want anything to do with our ministry if we supported John Kerry for president. I wrote back and told her that as a nonprofit ministry, we could not and would not promote any candidate. However, I also said to her, "You must understand that there are believers who will vote for John Kerry and those who will not, but together, Democrat and Republican, we have been called to work together to expand Christ's Kingdom around the world. We must work together even though we are different." I never heard from her again, so I don't know if she got the message or was upset with me!

In addition to the theological, administrative, and political differences, some believers just irritate us—they talk too much or too little; or they have one of a number of annoying habits, just as we do. However, we must learn to live with these differences because Christ and His Kingdom are more important to us than any inconsequential differences. Before telling us that there is only one Body, Paul says, *"As a prisoner for the Lord, then, I urge you to live a life worthy of the calling you have received. Be completely humble and gentle; be patient, bearing with one another in love. Make every effort to keep the unity of the Spirit through the bond of peace"* (Ephesians 4:1-3).

Paul has just prayed for the Ephesians (Ephesians 3:14-20), and it is important that we understand a bit about this prayer. Paul prays a number of things: 1) he prays that they will be strengthened in the core of their being by the indwelling Spirit; 2) he says when that happens, Christ will be established in their lives and they will be rooted in love; 3) when they are rooted in love, they will accept and respect different parts of the Body of Christ so that together they can see how high, wide, long, and deep God's love is; 4) they will be filled to the fullness of God; 5) God will do beyond their wildest imaginations. Because Paul prays about learning together and talks about unity after he tells them to walk worthy of the Lord, we must conclude that a worthy life for the Christian will include walking in the kind of unity with the entire Body of Christ that stimulates our personal growth. Paul then tells them—and us—how they—and we—can walk in this unity:

- *Be completely humble.* When we walk in humility, it means that we don't live life with our agenda always in view. We live to do what He wants us to do. Since God wants us to love one another, the person walking in humility will focus on others' needs. Paul told the Philippians that if they lived like that, they would be like Jesus (Philippians 2:1-5), who did not look to what He wanted, but served others, even to the point of dying for them. Humility also means once we know God's will for our lives, we will not try to do it by our own power. We understand that we can only do the will of God by the grace that He supplies. If we walk in humility, we will give our agenda to God, look to the interests of others, and then rely upon God's power to live out His will.

- *Be completely gentle.* He is telling the Ephesians to walk in meekness. Meekness is a Spirit-anointed ability to be moderate. Aristotle said that meekness is a way of life between "bad temper and spineless indifference."[1] In other words, we should not be rude or coarse with people. We can get that way with believers we think are not as spiritual as we are, or who have different beliefs. We can be condescending, like the young man in my first church who told me that when I was baptized in the Spirit, "I would understand." In other words, "When you get what I have, you will really get it." The truth is that I did need more of the Holy Spirit's power in my life, but the young man's attitude did not cause me to want to learn from him. We may have the ability to help someone, but if our attitude is not lovingly humble, they may not stick around long enough for us to help them.

- *Be patient.* We are patient when we are able to hang in there with people who don't seem to be making progress, or their progress is really, really slow. Instead of focusing on how slowly they are going, we need to see their potential and continue to help them as long as it takes, or until the Lord clearly gives us a new assignment. Isn't that what He does with us?

- *Bearing with one another.* We "bear with one another," when we "put up with" one another. Some people have quirks that are hard to deal with. They may have mannerisms that seem strange to us, or they have a difficult time understanding something that comes easy for us. Bearing with someone is a form of patience. When we bear with someone, we continue to work with them, in spite of the personal quirks. I remember being frustrated with my first associate pastor. He was always coming in late because he spent time talking with the people at the convenience store. I heard him on the phone laughing and talking all the time. He "wasn't working" like I was, digging into studies and spending time in prayer. I realized after he went to serve in another place that he was the opposite of me, a perfect match! I had gifts to teach and preach, and God had given him a love for people and a desire to be with them. If I had realized immediately what I understood later, the two of us would have accomplished more than we did, and I would have encouraged him to focus on being with people, where his gifts and potential resided.

Paul ends this passage by encouraging his readers to do everything to maintain unity through Jesus Christ. Unity is key to our evangelism and also our understanding of Christ, because we get greater revelation of Him from each other.

What about those doctrinal differences? We must admit that some of those doctrinal differences are troubling. I want to end this section by talking about how to handle differences in doctrines that do not fall into the absolutely essential core doctrines, like salvation in Christ.

- The differences may never change. We may have to live with the fact that we are working with genuine believers in Christ who have a heart to see His Kingdom advance and who are different from us. What do we do, in this case? I believe there are a couple of things to do: a) Continue to love each other. You can spend time together and pray for each other. b) Work together on projects that you feel comfortable working on together. You will continue to do things the way you do them, in your separate churches, but there are things you can do together. You can attend or start joint or regional prayer meetings, for example. You can participate in joint evangelistic efforts like a crusade or food ministry. c) Keep talking. You just might begin to understand each other.

- The differences that may never change, just might change. Later in Ephesians 4, Paul continues to talk about unity. He talks about the role of leaders preparing the people for their work of ministry. Paul says that this will happen:

  "...until we all reach unity in the faith and in the knowledge of the Son of God and become mature, attaining to the whole measure of the fullness of Christ. Then we will no longer be infants, tossed back and forth by the waves, and blown here and there by every

wind of teaching and by the cunning and craftiness of people in their deceitful scheming. Instead, speaking the truth in love, we will grow to become in every respect the mature body of him who is the head, that is, Christ" (Ephesians 4:13-15).

So often, we have believed that "speaking the truth" in love has to do with the way we confront someone. Of course if we confront someone, we should do it in love. Our desire is not to put them down, but to help them be more of what God wants. However, I believe this passage actually talks about the fact that as we love and respect one another in the Body of Christ, we will begin to gain an understanding of why other people hold the doctrinal positions that they do. When we begin to understand them, they may begin to understand us. This understanding will help us see strengths in the other person's position, and weaknesses in our own. We may both change a little and actually come closer to the truth, as God sees it. This means that we will be better able to communicate truth.

PRACTICAL WAYS TO LOVE ONE ANOTHER

What are some practical ways we can love each other in the Body of Christ? We have talked about some attitudes that must be present if we are going to walk in biblical love. Also we have discussed what to do when the differences are troubling. In this section, we want to talk about the nitty-gritty aspects of love. If we are not demonstrating our love in practical ways, do we really love?

1. *Shoulder each other's burdens (Galatians 6:2).* Paul told the Galatians that they should engage in bearing one another's burdens. Burdens come in many shapes and sizes. Let's discuss two of them and consider some suggestions.

Some believers may be burdened financially. Financial burdens come from many sources. Someone in the family may have lost a job, or there may be unexpected medical bills. When this happens, God may ask us to assist if we have the resources to help. James told the believers that saying "bless you" does not cut it when someone has a financial need and you have the ability to help (James 2:16). In fact, Paul indicates that the reason that some have been blessed is so they can give. He said to the Corinthian church when encouraging them to give, *"Our desire is not that others might be relieved while you are hard pressed, but that there might be equality. At the present time your plenty will supply what they need, so that in turn their plenty will supply what you need. The goal is equality"* (2 Corinthians 8:13-14).

On the other hand, some may be in financial difficulty because they have been unwise or sinful in some way, such as excessive purchases or gambling. In this case, you may want to give them money, but you may also help them develop a budget or help them overcome an addiction. God specifically tells us to help widows and orphans. These are ones who are unable to help themselves. Our situation today may be different. Some widows are well-fixed financially, but they may need help caring for their home or fixing the car. We may also include single moms in this category. We may assist orphans by sending money to ministries that care for orphans, or by adoption.

Some believers may have a burden because of sin. John tells us to pray for those engaging in sin (1 John 5:16), but I believe we can do more. I have had several men ask me to check in with them on pornography issues. We can pray and check up on our brothers and sisters in a caring, nonjudgmental way. This is love.

The actions mentioned are only two examples of the kinds of needs that members of the Body of Christ have. If you see a need, help if you can. I am not very mechanical. I can't fix things. In fact, when my wife thinks of me fixing something it scares her. However, I have a couple of Christian brothers who answer my car questions. One of them is willing to drive quite a distance to fix things for me. This is a great help to our ministry. When we leave on an international trip, one of our board members turns off the water and checks the house. He has the heat and water on and working when we get home so we can take a hot shower, after 30 to 40 hours on airplanes and in airports! This is such a blessing to us, and real love in action.

2. *You show love by helping brothers and sisters grow in their faith and helping them achieve their ministry goals (Hebrews 10:24-25).* There are a number of ways we can do this. Let us look at some of them.

Help other believers grow in their *spiritual life*. In Hebrews, Paul says, *"And let us consider how we may spur one another on toward love and good deeds, not giving up meeting together, as some are in the habit of doing, but encouraging one another—and all the more as you see the Day approaching"* (Hebrews 10:24-25). Helping in this way obviously involves many things. Considering the context, which we have already discussed, we know that Paul wanted these believers to spur one another out of their complacency that had caused them to shrink back from serving God passionately. Paul also calls us to spur one another to love and good deeds by helping to *build a foundation* in the lives of new believers. Each new convert must learn the truth, as recorded in the Scriptures, and must walk in the disciplines that we have talked about in the previous chapters. This is done best if we follow

Jesus' example. He built relationships with trustworthy believers and spent time with them. We will not have the ability to spend 24/7 time with them, but we can spend time training them. Eventually, we will involve them in ministry and help them discover their God-ordained destiny (see Chapter 14).

As we will discuss soon, spiritual leaders will train others to disciple new converts and oversee a process that will enable every believer who desires to fully follow God, to become a disciple of Christ. Since leaders cannot give time to everyone, each of us should look for ways to be involved in helping others learn what we have learned. This can be done by meeting with a person, a couple, or a small group. Small groups are a great way to help insure that believers continue to grow. They provide both love and accountability.[2]

The major way to help others grow is in the area of your *spiritual gifts.* The three passages often talked about in the area of spiritual gifts are: First Corinthians 12, Romans 12:1-8, and Ephesians 4:11-16. We will talk about the first two in more detail in the next chapter. For our purposes, I will merely say that when we come to the Lord and receive the Holy Spirit into our lives, God endows us with Spirit-empowered abilities that enable us to assist in advancing God's Kingdom. These gifts generally manifest in greater power when we are filled with or baptized in the Holy Spirit. Although we will help others in many ways, we will spend the majority of our ministry helping the Body by using our gifts. (More later.)

3. *God uses gifted spiritual leaders to oversee the process.* (Read Ephesians 4:11-16.) *"So Christ himself gave the apostles, the prophets, the evangelists, the pastors and teachers, to equip his people for works of service, so that the body of*

Christ may be built up" (Ephesians 4:11-12). As I said earlier, the leaders cannot spend a great deal of time with everyone, but Paul tells us that they are to oversee a process that will prepare people for their ministry. This includes three areas. First, they will be doing all they can to make sure that the believers under their charge become mature believers in Christ. When they preach and teach, they will teach principles that will help each believer become what God desires. They will also understand that this cannot be fully achieved from the pulpit. We grow when we have accountability, so leaders will train others who will train others, and so on (2 Timothy 2:2).

Second, leaders will help believers discover their spiritual gift(s) so they can be effective in their walk with the Lord. Third, they will set believers in their place of ministry. In most cases, this will begin by helping them find their place in the church or Christian organization to which they belong. At some point, it will mean releasing some of those who are trained to go into other ministries where they can be most effective. Some will serve on the staff of churches, others will become missionaries to the inner city or another country, and some may acquire jobs in other parts of the country or world where they will serve as God leads. God will call committed Christians in all these ways.

Sometimes, sports commentators talk about the greatness of a coach. One of the qualities they often discuss is how many assistant coaches they have trained who are now head coaches. God wants our spiritual leaders to be like that. Some of those we send out may become more successful than we are. This is our task.

4. *We can help those who are engaged in ministry.* I will talk primarily about those who are in vocational Christian service, but many of the principles apply to those who minister as a volunteer in local churches and ministries as well. The most important thing you can do for anyone in ministry, regardless how small, is to pray. My wife and I encourage every leader to have a prayer team. A number of years ago when we served in a difficult church, God led me to spend a number of afternoons alone with Him to seek Him for ways to make us more effective. During that time, He told me to get a group of people committed to praying for our family and ministry. Although there had been some pressures, things eased up a bit, and I did not follow through. A few months later, a pastor friend of mine went through a very dark time. At that same time, a young woman who had prayed for Kerry and me, said that God woke her up and told her that we didn't have sufficient prayer support. Because we had seen what my friend was going through, we immediately recruited and trained a group of people to pray for us. It made an amazing difference in our lives and ministry.

A second thing we can do for those in ministry is to see if there are ways we can help. When we went fulltime with KingdomQuest, a friend said she would be my volunteer secretary. This enabled me to focus on ministry, while she took care of administrative details. Eventually she moved thousands of miles away, but there are a number of things she did to increase the quality of our work, which we still do today. Third, we can give financially. Ministries need finances for more reasons than most of us can imagine. Things like accounting, insurances, and administrative costs. Then, of course, there are salaries, and the costs of doing the ministry which usually includes as travel.

IN SUMMARY

We have seen the great privilege we have to be part of a committed family. Therefore, look for a group of like-minded, fully committed believers with whom you can enter into genuine Christian fellowship. Be aware that it might not always be easy to live together with our quirks and differences. Ask the Lord to cement in your thinking that there is only one Body of Christ, and ask Him to work in your character to enable you to walk in unity. Last but not least, love others in a practical way. Help them become all that God wants them to be with every resource you have available to help them: time, finances, and spiritual gifts. As you do this, you will see God's Kingdom advance in your city and around the world.

ENDNOTES

1. Gerhard Kittel and Gerhard Friedrich, eds., translated and abridged by Geoffrey W. Bromiley, Theological Dictionary of the New Testament (Grand Rapids, MI: Wm. B. Eerdmans Publishing Co.), 930.

2. There are many good books about small groups. If you or your church desires to have a small group ministry, I suggest you read several and learn how they function. A couple of good ministries are Willow Creek in Chicago and Dove Fellowship in Ephrata, Pennsylvania.

CHAPTER 14

Discovering Your
God-Ordained Destiny

As I have studied the Gospel of John the past five years, I have found the end to be interesting and a bit confusing. Chapter 20 ends with John telling His readers why he wrote the Gospel. I suppose he waited until the end hoping that the readers would discover it on their own, but clarifies his purpose in writing in case his readers missed it. This seems to me like the perfect place to end the Gospel. However, there is more.[1]

In the last chapter of the Gospel, Jesus assures Peter that He loves him; Peter declares his love for Jesus, and Jesus tells Peter what his ministry will be. When Jesus told Peter to feed His sheep, He made Peter the leader of His disciples. This last chapter of the Gospel of John is a new chapter in the life of the church. Jesus left earth to go to His Father in heaven. Before He left, He commissioned the Church to continue His work of advancing His Kingdom, and He set Peter as their leader. So, we might say that John chapter 21 initiated the beginning of the Church age with its leader in place and the Church waiting for the promised Holy Spirit to empower them.

Peter must have been relieved and excited to receive Jesus' forgiveness and to understand that Jesus did not discard him, but had plans for him in the newly commissioned Church. Jesus not only had a plan for Peter, but He has a plan for every disciple who has committed their lives to Jesus. As we read the Book of Acts, which tells us about the early years of the Church, we find that God had a plan for every committed believer. Peter and Paul had both been called to be apostles, but Peter went to the Jewish people and Paul to the Gentiles; Stephen was a deacon; Philip was an evangelist; others supported the ministry financially and some served as elders. Each one played a role that helped advance the Kingdom. Paul told the Ephesians, *"For we are God's handiwork, created in Christ Jesus to do good works, which God prepared in advance for us to do"* (Ephesians 2:10).

Before we were born God had a plan for us filled with good works. Because He knew what He desired to do through us, He created everything about us with His plan in mind, even our physical and mental capacities. The story is told about Amy Carmichael, the great missionary to India, that when she was a little girl she asked God to change her brown eyes to blue when she went to bed. God never changed them. When Amy went to India, she would rub wet tea leaves on her face so it would be the color of the Indians she would see on the street. She would then go into crowds, where little girls were being trafficked and rescue them.[2] Had God given her blue eyes, those selling the girls would have recognized her as a Westerner. God knows best.

God has given each of us a purpose that enables us to play a part in taking His Kingdom to the ends of the earth. This last chapter has been dedicated to helping you discover God's purpose for your life and to assist you in fulfilling that purpose.

WHAT DO YOU HAVE TO OFFER?

Often when people are asked to help with a ministry, they respond by saying, "I would love to, but what do I have to offer?" Some may say, "I haven't been to Bible college or seminary. What can I do?" It is easy to think that we do not have much to offer, but each of us has been called to a specific purpose. Let's begin by discussing two similar but very different parables of Jesus that describe what each of us has to offer.

The Parable of the Minas (read Luke 19:12-27). A mina was a denomination of money, which equaled about three month's wages. The parable talks about a king who gave an equal denomination of money to three men. He instructed them to invest the money for him while he was away. The king rewarded two of the men who invested the money wisely. However, a third man did not do anything with the money and the king rebuked him. The important thing to note in this parable is that all three men received an equal amount of money. This symbolizes the resources that all believers possess equally. Each of us has been given twenty-four hours in a day as well as all the means of grace we have already discussed. Because Jesus has supplied these blessings, He expects us to utilize them so we can live as much like Him as possible and fulfill the purpose for which we exist.

The Parable of the Talents (read Matthew 25:14-30). At first glance, this parable looks like the exact same parable told at a different time. Each of three men had been given money to invest while their leader went on a journey. In each case, the men had been asked to invest the monies in order to make a profit. Two of the men invested wisely, and were rewarded, while a third man did not invest the money and received rebuke. Both parables tell us that we will someday give an account before God concerning how we lived our lives. This accounting, or judgment, will determine how effective each believer served the Lord after they received Him. Our heavenly rewards will be decided at that time.

There is a major difference in this parable, though, because these three men did not receive an equal amount of money. The first received five talents, the second two, and the third one talent. This parable tells us that God expects believers to use the unique resources that He has given them to advance the Kingdom of God. Note that even though the first two men did not begin with an equal number of talents and did not produce an equal number of talents, they received an equal commendation from their leader because they used what he had given them for His purposes. The same will be true of believers today, if we allow Him to use the gifts and talents that He has placed in us.

The unique resources that God gives us fall into four categories: spiritual gifts; natural birth talents; life experiences; and our unique calling.

I. SPIRITUAL GIFTS

(Read First Corinthians 12:7-11 and Romans 12:1-8.) When someone is born again, the person is given supernatural abilities that enable him or her to play a role in advancing the Kingdom of God. These are not the abilities that the person was born with, but abilities given by the Holy Spirit at the time of the believer's new birth. The abilities generally become more evident when the believer is filled with or baptized in the Holy Spirit. You will note that although every believer receives gifts of the Spirit, they do not all receive the same ones. Paul tells us that some have this gift and some have another. God wants us to discover the gifts He has given us so He can use us in ministry. Let's look at the gifts recorded in First Corinthians and Romans.

1 Corinthians 12

- Message of wisdom. Someone receives a message or word of wisdom when God supernaturally shows the person, or a group, how to proceed with a project or ministry. It is wisdom placed in the person's spirit directly from God.

- Message of knowledge. A message or word of knowledge occurs when God gives information to a believer that the person could not know if God had not revealed it. My pastor tells a story of a time when he was praying with people in the front of the church. As he was praying for a young man, he felt like the Lord told him to tell the young man, "You will amount to something, honey!" He obeyed God and said it. The young man broke into tears. It turned out that when the man's father was dying, he told the young man, "Honey, you will never amount to anything!" (Note: The father loved the son and was very sick and his mind was not functioning normally when he made the statement.) God used this word of knowledge to get the young man back on track in his life.

- Faith. We are all to live by faith. However, there are some who have an extra measure of grace to trust God for amazing things. George Mueller cared for thousands of orphans in England with little money, except what God supplied miraculously.[3]

- Gifts of healing. We can all pray for the sick and see them recover. As I mentioned earlier, God has used my wife and I in this area and we want to be used more. However, some have a gift of healing and regularly see individuals healed as they pray.

- Miracles. This gift is similar to healing only in areas not involving sickness. These believers regularly pray about impossible situations and see God answer. For instance, they may pray about the weather when it looks like an event ordained by God will need to be canceled.

- Prophecy. Prophecy fits into two categories. 1) Some believers have been gifted to preach messages based on the truths of Scripture, which call the church to repentance. When those with this gift preach, God brings repentance and life-change. 2) The second type of prophecy occurs when God tells one believer something that will happen or could potentially happen in the life of another believer. A man gifted in this way described Kristin's, my oldest daughter, future husband when she was still in high school. She did not know that Andrew existed. However, as we listened to that word of prophecy, the prophetic teacher described him perfectly.

- Tongues. Tongues occur when God gives a message to someone in a language that they do not know. This gift works in two ways. The first way that God will use the gift of tongues is to have a believer speak in a current or archaic language that he does not know. When this occurs, there is generally someone in the group who does understand the language. This type of tongue acts as a miracle that will help cause the person, recognizing the language being spoken in tongues, to be open to coming to Jesus.

Pastor Jack Hayford tells of a time when he sat next to a man on an airplane. The Lord told him to speak to the man in tongues, asking him if what he said was a language the other man knew. Pastor Jack did not know the language at all. It turned out to be perfect Koiwa Indian language. This incident caused the man, who had been closed to the Gospel, to become open.[4] The second way that God uses the gift of tongues occurs when a person speaks in tongues in a group meeting. When this occurs, there should always an interpretation of the message in tongues in the language common to those in the meeting.

This type of tongues is designed to get the attention of one or more persons in the meeting.

- Interpretation of tongues. This is the gift when someone interprets a message in tongues in a group meeting. The interpretation is very similar to a prophetic word in a public meeting.

Romans 12

- Prophecy. See previous section.

- Serving. Some call this the gift of helps. Those who possess this gift love to serve, often in the background. Their gift serves others well and often helps leaders perform their ministry without having to sweat the details.

- Encouragement. The person with this gift has the ability to help people keep going as they seek to fulfill the Lord's plan. It falls into two equally important categories. Those with this gift know how to do both. The first is lifting people out of discouragement. The one operating in this gift will say something like, "You can do it." Sometimes the person with the gift of encouragement will need to exhort another person. This can come in the form of rebuke. I remember a time when I was feeling sorry for myself. Pastor Waltimyer, whom I mentioned earlier, said, "John you're feeling sorry for yourself and it stinks!" That statement snapped me out of the doldrums. I made the mistake of telling my wife what Pastor Waltimyer said. So when I am feeling sorry for myself (nobody else will), she reminds me what he said. The person with the gift of encouragement will know when to use the gentle approach and when to exhort.

- Teaching. This gift is the ability to teach the Word of God in a way that the listeners understand the truth of God so it becomes revelation to them.

- Contributing to the needs of others or giving. Those who possess this gift are people who have a supernatural ability to give. They may have a lot of money, but it is not necessary. Our hairdresser does not have a lot of money, but she loves to give and she gives money and gifts to many people.

Each of us has been given one, and probably more than one, of these gifts. We should seek the Lord to see which gifts He has given us. I suggest three activities that may help you to discover your gifts:

1. Try things. When there is a need in a ministry, in your small group, or church, volunteer to help if it is something you can do. I can't sing very well, so I would not sign up to sing a solo. However, we can attempt most ministries. As you volunteer for a variety of ministries over a period of time, observe where God uses you. You will also often discover that you enjoy ministering in the area of your gifts.

2. Ask committed Christians who know you well to observe you and tell you where they believe God uses you and where they perceive your gifts to lie.

3. Take a Spiritual Gifts Inventory. I suggest that you wait until you have tried a number of ministries first, then take one of these tests. These tests generally are a series of questions that ask you to describe your experience and passion about certain areas of ministry. It will be difficult to answer properly if you have had little experience. The tests are very subjective, but will be much more accurate if you have some experiences to draw on. As you answer the questions, you gain a greater understanding of how God

has gifted you. Remember that He is not hiding them from you. He wants you to know, so He will make them clear to you in His time. When you begin to understand your gifts, the Holy Spirit will give you an inner peace about it.

2. NATURAL BIRTH TALENTS

God also gave you talents and aptitudes when you were born physically (Psalm 139:13-16). Each of us has been specifically made to fulfill a role by God. Scottish Olympic runner Eric Liddell had been called to be a missionary. However, he also ran in the Olympic games. When his sister questioned him about his running (because she questioned whether he should do so as a Christian), he admitted that God had called him to ministry; but, Liddell said, "He also made me fast."[5] Although Liddell became an effective missionary, God may have used his Olympic triumph to win even more people to Christ because his story and the story of sprinter Harold Abrahams was made into an Academy Award winning movie, *Chariots of Fire.* Christians in the U.S. invited many people to see the movie because it depicted Liddell's faith unabashedly. The movie became an effective evangelistic tool.

Your "natural birth talents" include every talent God gave you at birth. It might be business acumen, the ability to fix things, or other skills. These talents give believers a platform to witness or assist ministries. My wife's computer died recently. She needed a computer to keep in contact with our international family and U.S. partners. One day a wonderful believer who loves to work on computers showed up with a rebuilt computer, which is more than we could have anticipated. It is all she will need for quite some time. He did not charge our ministry a penny, which means we did not have to use monies we had set aside for future mission trips. This man has a talent and it has become a ministry. He not only rebuilds and gives computers away, but he travels to other countries helping missionaries and Bible colleges set up their computers and computer networks. He is using his birth talent to help advance the Kingdom of God. We are so grateful. Ask God to show you how your birth talents can help advance the Kingdom of God.

3. Life experiences

We all have unique life experiences. These experiences can help us minister to others. Some of these experiences come out of dark times in our lives. We may have struggled with some sin or unrighteous habit like alcohol addiction, drug use, or pornography. However, God has given us victory! God can use our experiences to relate to and help others in ways that those who have not gained victory cannot. Have you seen a rocky marriage healed? God can use that experience to help others. (Please hear me out. I am not saying that these things are good. I am saying that God's victory in your life is good and He can use your victory to help others.) Paul says God *"comforts us in all our troubles, so that we can comfort those in any trouble with the comfort we ourselves receive from God"* (2 Corinthians 1:4). Every victory we have won is part of the talent that God has given to us.

Each progression you make in becoming more like Jesus and every way you learn to minister are life experiences you can share with others. The Lord can use your close walk with the Lord, the effective way you tell others about Jesus, and the way you love folks in your neighborhood, at work, or at school. God wants you to use every victory and every inch of growth as tools to minister to others and advance the Kingdom.

4. Your unique calling

God has given us unique gifts, talents, and experiences so He can use us in our specific calling. Our calling represents the specific place that God wants to focus our ministry. For instance, I have the gift of teaching. There are many who have this gift. Some have been called to be Sunday school teachers, some teach in a seminary, and others may do what my wife and I do, which is challenging and training leaders to walk closely with God and to fulfill their God-ordained ministry. Some who have the gift of teaching may be able to teach children but not adults. I am the opposite. I can teach adults but am not as effective in teaching children. Our calling determines the specific place God wants us to use our gifts.

We have talked about how to determine our spiritual gifts and how God can use our birth talents and experiences to fulfill His will through us. We may discover more talents and gifts as we progress in life. God may not reveal all of our gifts right away. For instance, He may wait to reveal leadership gifts until we have gained some spiritual maturity. If we have not matured enough to lead with humility, we will sabotage our own ministry and the ministry of others.

We will certainly gain more life experiences as we move forward with the Lord. They will continue to help us relate to and help others. The computer story I told you earlier shows us once again that God supplies. However, our gratitude goes further. We would not have received this gift if another friend had not done some research and found the computer-giving ministry for us. We marvel at the goodness of God.

However, we now want to get into the area of calling. Obviously, we cannot be involved in every area of the Lord's work. So we must start by looking at the two overarching areas: local church ministry and missions. Within these two areas there are many different focuses to consider such as: Do I evangelize or teach? Do I engage in foreign compassionate ministries or rescue children from human trafficking? Then within these focused areas there are various positions like ministry support, leadership, and others.

So where does God want you to invest your efforts, time, talents, and gifts—by the power of the Holy Spirit? The following questions may help you:

- *Where is your passion?* God will place a passion in your heart. My wife and I are passionate in a couple of areas. We want to see the Church fulfill its destiny in God, but we also love to minister to different ethnic groups especially Pakistanis and Indians. We also care deeply about our persecuted brothers and sisters. These passions act as a compass pointing to the places we should allow God to use our gifts. So we want to minister in the U.S. and abroad, calling the Church to revival and mission. God's calling on others is different. A young couple from our church recently went to Thailand because they are passionate about rescuing girls from sexual exploitation. Some feel called to keep computers going for ministries. *What is your passion?*

- *What combination of gifts do you possess?* God often blesses His children with a number of spiritual gifts. The combination of these gifts or experiences may point us in the direction we should go. One of our dear friends has the gift of teaching, but she also possesses the gift of mercy. She loves to teach the Word of God to people who are "down and out." My wife has an ability to exhort people in such a way that they do not know they have been exhorted. They call her "the velvet brick." She exhorts as she teaches and people receive it gladly. If I said some of the things she does, they would throw tomatoes or worse at me. God leads others differently. If, for instance, you have the gifts of helps and mercy, God may call you to be part of a food ministry or some compassionate ministry. Passion combined with your gift mix will assist you in discovering your calling.

- *Where have you had difficulty?* Often God will give us a passion to see people overcome in areas that you had to overcome. Our pastor, David Hess, was miraculously healed of leukemia that should have killed him. He is passionate to see people healed.[6] An elder at a church, where we sometimes minister, served time in jail and had a debilitating problem with drugs. He is now a local leader with a drug rehabilitation ministry. He is passionate to see individuals get clean and come to Jesus.

- *Ask others what they perceive as your calling.* When I mentioned to Reverend Waltimyer that I thought God was calling me to be a pastor, he said, "I think you are on to something." Others may see your calling before you do. I suggest that you begin by asking someone in your church's leadership. One of the roles of leaders in the church is to help build a foundation in the lives of those under their care, but they also provide guidance in assisting each one to find their spot in God's Kingdom army.

Now That You Know

What should you do when you believe you are being led by God concerning your spiritual gifts—and possibly your life calling? I offer the following suggestions to answer that question:

1. ***Continue to develop in the basics of Kingdom living discussed in the first thirteen chapters in this book.*** We must continue to grow in these basic areas. As both demands and opportunities grow in our ministry, we need to grow deeper roots into Jesus so we will grow in our character and develop a deeper anointing for ministry because many more demands will be placed upon us and the enemy will resist our efforts even more.

2. *Look for ways to grow in your gifts and callings.*

- Having a *mentor* is a great place to begin. Find a gifted believer, in your congregation or who lives nearby, who has had fruitful experience in the areas of ministry where you feel called. A mentor will help you develop your gifts and give you feedback in many areas in your life. He or she will assist you in character development and guide you in pursuing ministry, often helping you avoid pitfalls.

- *If you cannot find a mentor nearby, read books by people who can assist you.* In our first, very small church, my wife spent a great deal of time reading books written by a few select pastors' wives, whom she respected. Reading these books helped her greatly. They were her mentors. In fact, even if you have a mentor, reading is helpful. Ask your mentor what books have had the most profound impact on his or her life.

- *Attend conferences and take classes.*

- *In some cases, you many need to get some type of ministry school diploma or seminary degree.*

3. *Continue to be open to God unveiling more of His plan for your life.* After serving in pastoral ministry for eight years, God called me to go to seminary. This experience helped develop me and the gifts He gave me. It was His plan for me. Then after serving in pastoral ministry for twenty-nine years, God called my wife and me to travel and train leaders. Who knows what is next!

He has similar surprises for each of us that will propel us forward toward fulfilling His plan for our lives. I urge you to *never stop grow-*

ing in character and ministry. God's Kingdom is ever-expanding—not only in the world, but also in our lives. Let's go for everything God has for us so we may bring Him the greatest glory!

IN SUMMARY

God has provided each of us many resources to fulfill His will for our lives. He has given us His grace to enable us to become increasingly like Jesus. He has also called us to a specific ministry and has given us birth talents and spiritual gifts, which give us the "skills" to fulfill that calling by the power of the Holy Spirit. In addition, we have life experiences that demonstrate the faithfulness and power of God in our lives that provide us with opportunities to minister to those who are hungry for change. God has also given us passions that show us where we should use our gifts.

In order to fulfill all that God would have you do, I suggest the following:

1. Continue to grow to Christian maturity. If you are new in Christ, focus on growing. Particularly develop a close personal relationship with the Lord. Learn the basics: Learn how to pray; Get to know the Bible; Hang out with like-minded, committed Christians; and get involved in ministry in every way you can. God will soon show you where He wants you to begin ministry.

2. Meet with mature believers who can help you become all you were designed to be.

3. Try things to discover your spiritual gifts.

4. Do what you can to develop your gifts.

5. Observe what you are passionate about and ask God how He can use this in ministry.

ENDNOTES

1. I know the Gospel was not divided into chapters when John wrote the Gospel. However, he did write more after he told them the meaning of his Gospel. This indicates to me that he had a very important point in writing what we call the last chapter.

2. I don't have the exact reference, but heard the story told through the teachings of Child Evangelism Fellowship.

3. Read more on George Muller in Basil Miller's book: *George Muller: Man of Faith and Miracles* (Ada, MI: Bethany House Publishers, 1972).

4. Jack Hayford, *The Beauty of Spiritual Language* (Dallas, TX: Word Publishing, 1992), 75-82.

5. *Chariots of Fire;* 1991 British movie that won best picture award at the Academy Awards. The film was conceived and produced by David Puttnam, written by Colin Welland, and directed by Hugh Hudson.

6. See Dave Hess's story in his book *Hope Beyond Reason* (Shippensburg, PA: Destiny Image Publishers, 2008).

Conclusion

We have discussed much in this book. It is not possible to take it all in during one reading. I suggest you ask God which areas He wants you to work on now. This will alleviate the feeling that you need to do it all this month.

I remember attending a conference for young pastors seeking to be ordained. There were four seminars led by four pastors, each greatly gifted in the topic they taught that day. I was so discouraged. I thought, *I can't do **one** of these things as effectively as these presenters, how am I going to do them **all?*** A friend said, "John, if you take one thing away from this day that will help you in your life and ministry, it will have been a success."

Therefore, I encourage you not to become discouraged if you have not mastered everything in this book. There is room for growth in every Christian—right up until the day we pass into heaven. Therefore, ask God:

- Which area(s) do You want me to work on, Lord?

- In what priority should I start working on them?

- What specific strategies for each area will help me grow best?

- Who would be a good accountability partner, someone who will help me grow and hold me accountable?

I suggest you read and re-read the book and discuss it over a period of time with a men's or women's group or Sunday school class. The book has not been written just to give more information, but to help you become all that God desires of you—fulfilling your God-given destiny as you enjoy life being *fully alive*. As our Indian and Pakistani friends say, "Happy journey!"

APPENDIX A

How are We Doing?

If He has given us grace to live differently, there ought to be results that confirm that the Church is doing well. For this reason, it is fair to ask how the Church has done since Jesus went back to be with the Father. What has the church accomplished in the last 2000 years? Operation World has put together a book, CD and website to assist the Church to understand how to pray for the advance of God's Kingdom. They also tell us how the Church is doing around the world. The editors have done painstaking research to give accurate information. Much of the information we will list below comes from it. In 2010, there were about 6.9 billion people in the world. Of those, one in three considers himself to be a Christian.[1] This includes those who consider themselves Christian in any way. However, we find that a full half of those claiming to be Christians fall into the evangelical, charismatic, Pentecostal (I will call them ECP) branches of the Church,[2] indicating that a minimum of half the church has a focus on evangelism and missions.

This figure represents 1/6th of the world's population.[3] Africa has moved from 7.5 million believers in 1900 (about 9.1 percent) to 504 million in 2010 (48.8 percent).[4] Latin America has 546 million who claim to be Christians or 49 percent of the total population. Nearly half fall into the ECP camps.[5] In North America, which includes Canada, Central America, Mexico and the United States, over half claim to be part of the ECP branch of the Church.[6] In Australian, 34.5 percent claim to be ECP.[7] The statistics for Asia and Europe are not as encouraging. In Asia, just fewer than 9 percent claim to be Christian and about 6 percent ECP[8] and in Europe about 10 percent claim Christianity with 5 percent ECP.[9]

God, however, is working even in these difficult places. A Chinese pastor who oversees a House Church Movement, told us that there are 70 million believers in China. This is amazing since there were only tens of thousands when the missionaries were deported in the middle of the 20th Century.[10] One source that may not be as reliable as Operation World tells us that 17% of India may be Christian. This is much higher than the official statistics, but demonstrates that headway is being made.[11] Jerry Trousdale tells us that there may be 1 million Muslims coming to Christ each year in Africa.[12] He continues by telling us that between 2005 and 2012 six thousand churches have been planted among Muslims, 45 unreached groups now have 3000 churches among them and hundreds of former Sheikhs are leading movements for Jesus.[13]

We still have much work to do. Over two-thirds of the world still needs Jesus, but obviously millions have latched a hold of the grace of God, and have consistently lived the life that God intended for them. THIS TIME IT REALLY HAS BEEN DIFFERENT! WE HAVE GREAT HOPE THAT WE CAN FULFILL THE GREAT MISSION OF GOD BECAUSE OF JESUS!

ENDNOTES

1. Jason Mandryk, Operation World(Colorado Springs: Biblical Publishing, 2010), p. 2

2. ibid. page 3

3. I recognize that not all falling in ECP are truly born again and evangelizing, and that many in other parts of the Body of Christ have vibrant relationships with him. I am using these statistics to help us understand that God has many servants seeking to advance His Kingdom and many in the ECP groups are engaged in Kingdom Advance.

4. ibid. page 33

5. ibid. page 47

6. ibid. page 43

7. ibid. pages 84-85

8. ibid. 58

9. ibid. 74

10. Pastor Jack (not his real name) visiting and preaching at New Love in Christ Church in Harrisburg, PA in July 2013

11. wiki.answers. com/ What is the percentage of Christians in India? Accessed 12/10/2013

12. Jerry Trousdale Miraculous Movements (Nashville: Thomas Nelson, 2012), page 24

13. ibid. page 15

About
KingdomQuest Ministries

KingdomQuest Ministries (KQM) exists to be a catalyst to assist the Body of Christ in fulfilling the Great Commission throughout the earth. John and Kerry Shuey, founders of KQM, are called to equip others to advance Christ's Kingdom through seminars, preaching in churches, mentoring and the writing of materials. In their quest to fulfill this mission, they have ministered in many nations and parts of the U.S.

The Shueys have a burden to see the Body of Christ united in her quest to advance the name of Jesus throughout the world. As such, they attempt to have leaders from as many parts of the Body of Christ as possible at their meetings, and to see women elevated to their rightful place in ministry.

They also desire to see every individual Christian and congregation discover their God-ordained destiny. In order to assist believers and congregations, they have written two previous training manuals: *Breaking Free to Your Destiny*, which helps individual believers to break free of their past so they can walk into the destiny that God has for them, and *Becoming You*, which assists believers to discover and live out their destiny in God.

The Shueys have a great burden for the Persecuted Church, and a desire to see Muslims come to Christ. They engage in a wide variety of seminars such as: "The Plight and Potential of Women"; "The Challenges and Opportunities Presented by Islam"; "Kingdom Marriage"; "Prayer"; "Breaking Free to Your Destiny"; "Becoming You"; "The Persecuted Church"; "The Cost of Discipleship and other Discipleship Seminars"; and others. They love to minister in regional, denominational and congregational ministries, and can be contacted at shueyconsult@yahoo.com.

To order more copies of
this book please to go to
https://www.createspace.com/4941644

Made in the USA
Middletown, DE
20 September 2015